CRIMINALS, COURTS AND CONFLICT

A Study of Crime and Litigation in Fourteenth Century Coventry

Arthur Gooder

Edited by Trevor John
With a memoir of Arthur Gooder by Peter Searby

Contents

List of Illustrations

Acknowledgements

I am truly grateful for the good offices of several people who have gladly helped to bring Arthur's paper into the light of day: Roger Vaughan, Coventry Arts and Heritage Officer, who paved the way for its appearance under the aegis of the City Archives; Mr. Leslie Hulton, who unasked, took on the formidable task of transferring typescript to wordprocessor; Dr. Trevor John, who has tailored the whole essay into an acceptable state, and Dr. Peter Searby with his sympathetic and perceptive appreciation of Arthur. I also owe cordial thanks to Professor Peter Coss, who put out considerable, though unavailing effort to find an outlet for this study.

Finally, thanks to Susan Worrall, Coventry City Archivist and John Ementon, Graphic Designer, Cultural Development Design and Display Office for all their effort in seeing this work through to publication.

Eileen Gooder

Arthur Gooder, 1909-1992:
some memories and impressions

Criminals, Courts and Conflict was written in Arthur Gooder's retirement, in the secluded cottage deep in the Warwickshire countryside where he lived for almost half his life. A few hundred yards from a busy Midlands road along which he often travelled to his extramural classes, Oak Tree Cottage was a green and leafy retreat for Arthur and his wife Eileen. Its serenity would immediately envelop me on the frequent visits that began nearly forty years ago. Chatting in their sitting-room I was conscious of Arthur's burly frame and Eileen's slighter figure. He possessed an unobtrusive confidence in his talents, and was comfortable with himself and relaxed with others, while preserving an old-fashioned formality in social relationships; not until we had known each other for five years did he suggest that we might address each other by our first names.

Arthur was a keen and good-humoured observer of the social comedy. His anecdotes would begin quietly and then gradually engage all his energies. As his eyes sparkled a deep-throated laugh would begin and then move out of control; his body would shake and his right leg, crossed over his left, would joggle rhythmically. When spasms of laughter seized him while he was driving he would rock back and forth until the car itself, most likely an ancient Riley (Arthur was a friend to proven technology) would start to rock and then slow down, to the irritation of motorists following him. He tended not to notice. He was less selfconscious than most of us: you always felt that you were meeting the genuine Arthur.

In the background, as we sat in Oak Tree Cottage, was the ticking of a distant clock that marked the divisions of the day for two dedicated scholars. The walls were lined with a medley of books - history, poetry, novels - which were shelved in the slight and pleasing disorder that suggested frequent use. Through the windows one could see a subtle and harmonious garden of three quarters of an acre that the Gooders had created from a wilderness; it was especially the product of Eileen's enthusiasm, and she tends it still. A visitor used to suburban patches is struck by its rich and refreshing abundance.

Arthur was a Yorkshireman, born in 1909. West Riding inflections could be heard in his speech more than forty years after he left the county. Beneath the gentle and considerate demeanour there was a determination to stick to the path he had chosen; his obstinacy, rarely visible, surprised close friends when they glimpsed it. Part of him was hidden. Arthur came from Middlestown, between Wakefield and Huddersfield. His father, Allen, was a joiner, working mostly in the building trade and occasionally in collieries; he was shorter than Arthur, who inherited his large frame from his grandfather. Allen Gooder believed in education and enthusiastically supported Arthur, his only child; the two men were close. Arthur's self-effacing mother was a lesser influence.

After the local elementary school Arthur went to Ossett Grammar School on a scholarship; his size deterred anyone tempted to bully him. Another scholarship took him to Leeds University in 1928. At first he registered to read French, but was unhappy in it, in part, it is said, because his accent remained irredeemably West Riding; at all events he transferred to history after one term. In it he excelled, inspired by the great Leeds teachers A.S. Turberville and A. Hamilton Thompson. He had time for recreations, among them being cross-country running and cricket; Arthur was a left-handed batsman, an idiosyncrasy one would not have predicted, since he was normally right-handed. He also enjoyed country dancing. This pursuit brought friendship with Eileen McChesney, who graduated with a First in Latin in 1934; they married in December 1939.

After Arthur gained a First in history in 1931 he registered for a Ph.D., a very unusual venture in the 1930s. His doctorate was awarded in 1933, two years being then the minimum period of study required in Leeds. It is three years now, as in other universities, and to complete a doctoral thesis within that time is, we all know, a pretty rare feat. Arthur's achievement seems all the greater when one reads his thesis, The Parliamentary Representation of the County of York 1258-1832. The span of time Arthur covered, which in the 1990s everybody would regard as inappropriately long for a thesis, was not unique in the 1930s, though still uncommon. But it was customary then to draw upon a more limited range of sources than today. In contrast, Arthur's range of authorities, manuscript and published, would now be regarded as thorough for a dissertation dealing with just one generation. His thesis shows what Arthur could accomplish when he chose, while setting the pattern for the sort of research that he was to be attracted to for more than fifty years: creating mosaics from a mass of particulars, and so placing in our memory people and communities that would otherwise have been hidden from us. The outstanding contribution that he had made to scholarship was recognised by the publication of his dissertation in two volumes in the Yorkshire Archaeological Society's series, in 1935 and 1938.

At any time later than the 1930s Arthur's success would have been followed by a university post. During the Slump he taught in an all-age village school in Netherton, east of Middlestown; when he and Eileen married they moved to Wakefield, and Arthur began to teach at a senior school, taking children aged between eleven and fourteen, at Whitwood Mere between Castleford and Pontefract. Arthur cycled to school from Wakefield, fifteen miles each way. In the late 1930s he taught WEA classes too.

After a period as an air raid warden early in the war, in August 1941 he volunteered for the army. He served in the Royal Artillery as a gunner/signaller in the Eighth Army, fighting in the Western Desert, at the battle of El Alamein, and in the bitter Italian campaign. On 13 July 1944 at the battle for Monte Cedrone he displayed what his regimental record describes as 'exemplary courage', for which he was awarded the Military Medal, a fact to which in conversation he never referred. It is typical of Arthur's self-effacing quality that his comrades were apparently unaware of his scholarly talents. He remained in the ranks, though had he possessed the conventional amount of material aspiration he would without doubt have been given a commission. However, somebody in the War Office knew about him, and in February 1945 he was transferred to the Army Education Corps with the rank of captain; tantalisingly, the only information to hand about his activities in the AEC is that he produced Androcles and the Lion.

For a few years at the end of the Second War there was a mood of idealism in Britain - it seems hard to recapture it now - about the need to justify the loss and sadness of war by the creation of a better world; its chief result was the election of a Labour Government in 1945. Eileen has said about Arthur that he was 'dyed in the wool Labour: but he was not a political activist'. That chimes with my own memories; during our conversations he never responded to my youthfully partisan opinions. But that he shared the idealism of 1945 may be surmised from a poem he wrote after the battle of El Alamein. It is instinct with the need to preserve memory, and it contrasts the thoughts of the fortunate ones, like him, who survived the battle, with the words of those who died:

> quietly, as ordinary men, we passed,
>
> accepting with clear minds high risk of death.
>
> That henceforth men might live, we died, ye live;
>
> make ye our death worth while.

Arthur's lasting sense of mission deepened the historian's imperative, and in 1946 he was given an opportunity to convey to others the satisfactions of the past, when he was appointed to the Extramural Department of Birmingham University as a resident tutor responsible for north Warwickshire. Besides teaching, the post entailed much administration; Arthur had to organise classes taught by others, and to negotiate with local education authorities and the WEA. A valued tutor, Arthur was in the course of time promoted to a senior lectureship, and in the last five years of his service, from 1968 to 1973, he became a subject tutor, and was thus relieved from administrative labours that were becoming burdensome.

When Arthur came to north Warwickshire the prosperity of car manufacturing in Coventry in the preceding quarter of a century had led to the rapid growth of many old-established communities and the influx of many immigrants from other parts of Britain. Change aroused an interest in the past among newcomers and natives alike. Arthur realised that his classes wanted not 'England in Tudor times, but Warwickshire in Tudor times'. That assessment was consistent with his own predilections, and until he retired in 1973 he guided generations of adult students pursuing their roots in the home acres or pleasure in new surroundings into the meticulous gratifications of local history.

Arthur was a teacher of great quality but an unusual type. There was no hint of the dramatic gift that impels so many in the classroom. His sessions were undemonstrative, yet fascinating to the committed. On a typical evening ten students would be gathered round a table, each transcribing a document from the medieval or early modern centuries. Arthur would move from one to another, patiently elucidating difficulties; after half an hour he would talk to the group as a whole for about twenty minutes, about common concerns and the growth of the tapestry to which they were contributing their individual threads. Occasionally he would teach palaeography with Eileen, whose Latin for Local History (1961) is one of those rare books whose invaluable quality lasts for many decades. One student who attended a weekend school about 1975 (after Arthur's retirement from full-time university service) recalls their infectious enthusiasm, and their quiet yet firm expectation that the hours would be filled with hard work, as indeed they were.

The way in which Arthur's classes sometimes led to historical writing is shown by Plague and Enclosure: A Warwickshire Village in the Seventeenth Century, a substantial paper of some sixty pages published in 1965 by the Coventry Branch of the Historical Association. It investigates the fortunes of the village community of Clifton-on-Dunsmore through the vicissitudes of bubonic plague in 1604 and the enclosure of the open fields fifty years later, and is based on the work of an extramural class which met for some years at the Percival Guildhouse in Rugby. Under Arthur's direction the class transcribed the papers of two gentry families, the Townsends and the Bradfords, and also probate inventories at Lichfield. From the parish register it was possible to reconstruct the progress of the plague in 1604. The enclosure map was in part re-created by the class too, from maps of three different centuries in the Warwick Record Office. (Photocopies aided all this work, naturally.) The importance of Arthur's direction of these manifold tasks towards a common goal is clear; to the paper he also contributed much background knowledge and information gleaned from the Public Record Office and elsewhere. The result of all these endeavours remains a classic of local agrarian history, fit to be compared to The Midland Peasant and in places, indeed, superior to Hoskins's volume in the richness of its detail. Another example of Arthur's skill and patience in creating history of lasting stature from the labour of many hands is 'The Population Crisis of 1727-30 in Warwickshire', published in Midland History in Autumn 1972 (vol. 1, no. 4).

In both the pieces that I have cited Arthur names the members of the extramural classes concerned, and his words leave no doubt of his sense of obligation to them and his desire to requite their efforts fully. It is therefore puzzling that sometimes Arthur's part in this joint enterprise, the writing itself, was not completed with sufficient expedition. The most salient case is his study of the Black Death in Coventry. This is based on a large cache of deeds which extramural classes transcribed in the 1960s. In 1968 Arthur gave a paper on it to the Coventry Branch of the Historical Association. In my nine years in Coventry I heard many good lectures in the Herbert Art Gallery, some of them by world-famous historians. Arthur's was the one I remember best. Delivered in a gentle, intimate and often hesitant way which engaged the audience in a joint search for the past, it revealed the enthusiasm Arthur had brought to the re-creation of a medieval community: commitment to the rescuing of people that would otherwise be lost to us had carried him through years of painstaking effort. We glimpsed the passion that lay behind his calm exterior. It was one of those rare evenings that make local history a life-enhancing pursuit.

The lecture was as ready for publication then as any piece of historical writing ever is. The Dugdale Society was eager to publish it as an occasional paper. Arthur declined, feeling that more remained to be discovered in the Public Record Office; he spent much of the following quarter-century adding to the essay's detail, and like this study it has been published posthumously. Criminals, Courts and Conflict draws on the work of Arthur's students; but it contains so much of his own research that it should be regarded as only remotely connected with his teaching, having been subject to even more subtle and time-consuming elaboration than The Black Death. The usual explanation for the bent for procrastination that Arthur showed is 'perfectionism': but the word gives only the semblance of an answer. Historians know that research is never finished: at some time one must feel satisfied with what is only partly completed. When authors endlessly delay one tends to think that lack of self-assurance is responsible; but Arthur had no lack of that, and there was not a hint of the awkwardness or bluster that insecurity brings. Perhaps the truth was that Arthur was in need of the usual allocation of worldly ambition, and yet was also more sanguine than most of us, who know - especially after we reach sixty - that time is limited. Perhaps in part because his health had always been perfect, Arthur seemed to feel that life would go on for ever: one day his work would be ready for the printer, and meanwhile another journey to a record office would bring more threads to be added to the tapestry. The accumulation of detail was itself sufficient homage to the past he wished to preserve. One might say that for Arthur Gooder the journey not the arrival mattered.

In his last years he was working on yet another study, concerning Coventry in the late fourteenth century; and as preparation for it he was assembling on 4,000 index cards, from the sources he knew so well, biographical material about a multitude of Coventrians. There is something heroic about starting in old age a project that would daunt most people in their youth: one is reminded of Verdi composing Otello when he was eighty. But though the index cards will be a valuable resource for historians in generations to come, the new paper was not completed. It is baffling that Arthur did not see the wisdom of first drawing to a conclusion, during the brief span before him, essays which were so nearly ready and which people had long been hoping for. At all events he was adding to his index cards one morning in January 1992 when he was called into the next room for lunch. He took a few mouthfuls, sat back, and slipped away.

Peter Searby

Editor's Foreward

Most of the text of this study is as Dr. Gooder left it. It is a fine example of his industry and scholarship: how from a wealth of sources, both manuscript and printed, he has evoked not only the various jurisdictions which maintained law and order in fourteenth century Coventry, but also the texture of life, not always easily captured for this period, in that great medieval city. I have re-arranged the order of the text in a few places: most notably I have moved the biographies of the prior's and corporation's coroners to appendices to the chapters on their offices, so that they can be referred to as and when the reader feels appropriate. Some of the chapter headings and sub-headings are mine, inserted as sign-posts to guide the reader through a complex subject. I have written a short introduction to the chapter on the Cheylesmore courts, the area which is perhaps the most difficult for the layman to understand, and added a glossary. The list of sources has been recast. Otherwise, apart from a few minor corrections, what is here is pure Arthur Gooder.

I am grateful for the help and encouragement I have received from Eileen herself, and from Roger Vaughan, who has updated the references to documents in the Coventry City Achives. My task would have been much more burdensome but for the word processing abilities of Leslie Hulton. Mary Hulton has advised me on some infelicities of expression. The production of this memorial publication has enabled me to collaborate with my friend and former colleague, Peter Searby. I think it would have pleased Arthur to bring this group of people together in a common enterprise.

For readers who wish to see the subject in a wider social and geographical context, there are the following studies.

J. Bellamy, Crime and Public Order in England in the Later Middle Ages, London 1973.

J.G. Bellamy, The Criminal Trial in later medieval England. Felony before the Courts from Edward I to the Sixteenth Century, Stroud 1998.

B.A. Hanawalt, Crime and Conflict in English Communities, 1300-1348, Havard 1979.

B.A. Hanawalt, The Ties that Bound. Peasant Families in Medieval England, Oxford 1986.

R.F. Hunnisett, The Medieval Coroner, Cambridge 1961.

Trevor John
Kenilworth 1998

Trevor John

In 1965 Trevor John came from Lincolnshire, where he had been a senior history master in a grammar school, to join the staff of the Coventry College of Education. He was appointed to teach history to trainee teachers and to advise them on teaching the subject to children. These remained the major strands of his work when the College merged with the University of Warwick in 1978, and he was appointed a lecturer in what became the Institute of Education. In 1966 Arthur Gooder had recruited him to teach local history to adult extramural classes, and he developed particular interests in the medieval peasantry and the Civil War in the Midlands. These culminated in the publication in 1992 of *The Warwickshire Hundred Rolls of 1279-80* (British Academy, Records of Social and Economic History New Series XIX), based in his Ph.D thesis supervised by Professor Rodney Hilton, and his Coventry Historical Association pamphlet *Coventry's Civil War* (1994). He retired in 1997.

Peter Searby

Peter Searby taught history in Coventry from 1959 to 1968, first at Caludon Castle School and from 1962 at the College of Education. Active in the Historical Association, he was the first editor of its local history pamphlets, also the author of two titles in the series. In 1965 he registered at the newly founded University of Warwick as a research student of Edward Thompson, an association which he counts as his greatest good fortune as an historian. He has written much of Victorian Coventry, the theme of his Ph.D thesis, and though he still feels at home in the city regrets the passing of the nineteenth-century townscape he knew forty years ago. From 1968 until his retirement in 1994 he taught in the University of Cambridge, where he was Fellow of Fitzwilliam College. Among his recent publications is *A History of the University of Cambridge*: volume 3, 1750-1870 (Cambridge University Press, 1997).

John Speed's Map of Coventry, 1610.
Reproduced from an engraving made by W. Hollar for Dugdale's
Warwickshire, 1656.
Reproduced courtesy of Coventry City Libraries

Introduction -
The Local Jurisdictions in Coventry

In February 1370 two of the king's justices, Thomas de Ingelby and John Cavendish, arrived in Coventry to 'deliver' the gaol by presiding over the trials of the prisoners there. Awaiting their fate were five men charged with felonies - offences punishable by death. For those charged with serious offences, trial before the itinerant judges was the final stage in the judicial progress towards either hanging or outright acquittal, but while the five accused were all in the same situation, they had reached it by several routes. Three had been indicted before the Coventry justices of the peace: Adam Muleward, probably a miller, accused of stealing two shillingsworth of flour and oatmeal, John de Suffenhale, butcher, charged with stealing tallow, and Simon Blome, also a butcher, and owner of the disputed tallow, but before the court for sheep stealing. Only Suffenhale was in no danger of execution as the tallow in question was worth less than a shilling. Robert de Whatton, on the other hand, charged with homicide, had been indicted before the town coroner, while another alleged sheep-stealer, John le Shepherd, had appeared before the steward of Cheylesmore manor at the court leet held at Wolfpitlidyate, probably because the theft was said to have been from Stoke, outside the city. None of the accused at this gaol delivery had been indicted in the town court of the mayor and bailiffs, but this was another regular route to gaol and eventual trial. When the judges Grene and Skipwith came to deliver the gaol in September 1358, for instance, the two alleged coiners and a supposed horse-thief who awaited trial had all been through the mayor and bailiffs' court.

The juries acquitted all these accused, but our interest at this point is not in their fortunes, but in the local courts which had indicted them, and especially in what their records reveal of life in fourteenth century Coventry. While their power to punish serious crime was limited, their combined range was wide, covering minor offences and litigation between citizens, so touching the everyday business of the law-abiding as well as the transgressions of the dishonest and violent.

Part 1: The Coroner

Chapter 1: The Coroner in Action

While, as we have seen, indictments for felonies could originate in several courts, proceedings in cases of homicide normally began before the Coventry Coroner. On the finding of a body he apparently moved swiftly. The next day or the day after, even sometimes the same day if we believe the Coroners' Rolls, a jury was assembled and sworn, viewed the corpse and gave their verdict, naming the killer or outlining the circumstances of accidental death.[1] The victims could then be buried, and the coroner ordered the arrest of the killer and anyone suspected of helping or sheltering him. He then prepared an indictment on which the accused would be tried on the next visit of the justices of gaol delivery, if the bailiffs or others had managed to arrest them. From then on the law took its more leisurely course.

The coroner's office has been one of the more durable of English institutions, with a continuous history since 1194, when Richard I's itinerant justices were ordered to see that four 'keepers of the pleas of the crown' were elected in each county.[2] These coroners ('crowners'), as they soon came to be called, were responsible for ensuring that cases which should be reserved for the royal justices and not tried in the local courts were actually brought before the judges when they next visited the county. The first coroners were county officials, but large towns and the lords of liberties soon began to secure the right to have their own. In Coventry, Prior William Brightwalton, having united the city under the Priory by his purchase of the lordship of the Earl's part, obtained a royal charter in 1267 giving him the right to set up a merchant guild and also to have his own coroner in the town.[3] The Prior's move led to riots,[4] and nothing more was heard of the merchant guild, but from then on, Coventry had its own coroner.[5] However, when the men of the Earl's part had thrown off the Prior's lordship and secured their charter of incorporation, they bargained with Queen Isabella that she would purchase for them from the king the right to have a coroner.[6] Edward III made the grant in 1346[7] and for at least three years there were two coroners, the Prior's in his much-reduced

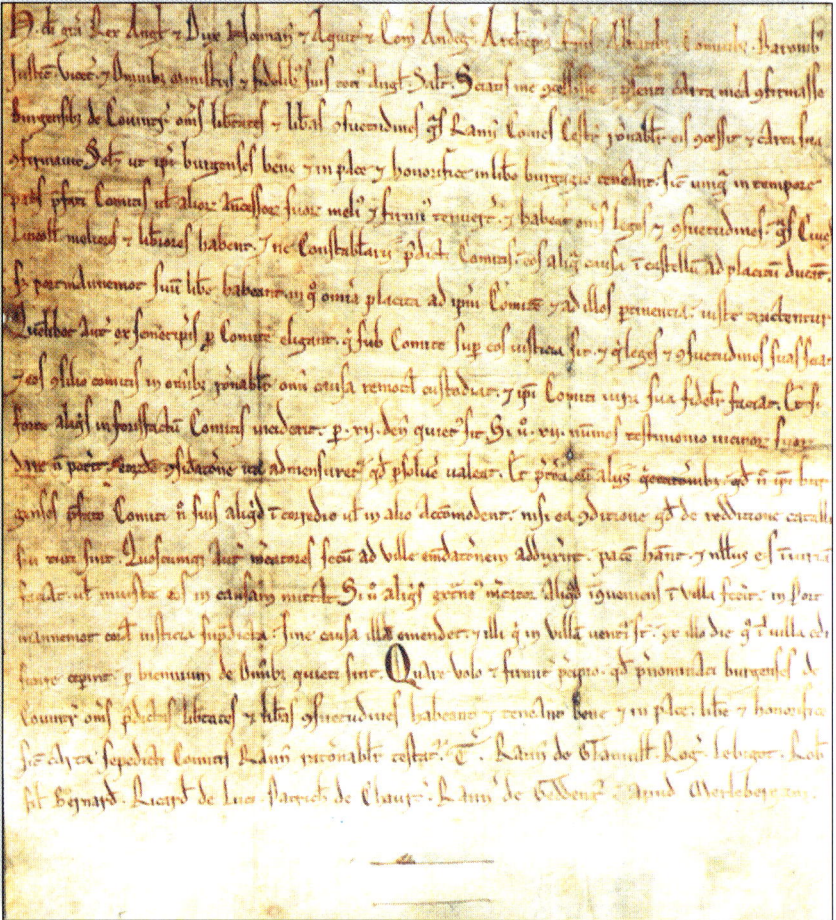

Charter of Henry II, 1182.

The earliest surviving Coventry Charter. Written in Latin on parchment, the citizens of Coventry paid 20 marks (£13 6s 8d) for it sometime between January and March 1182. It actually confirms a charter (which has not survived) granted between 1149 and 1153 by Ranulf de Gernon, Earl of Chester to the inhabitants of his 'half' of Coventry. The main provisions of Ranulf's charter were to confirm the rights already enjoyed by his tenants, and to grant them their own court (a 'portmote') and a justice elected from amongst themselves. It also promised merchants from elsewhere bringing goods into the town that they would be allowed to trade in peace, and granted newcomers exemption from taxation for two years after they started to build houses in the town. BA/H/A/1/1. *Reproduced courtesy of Coventry Archives.*

4

Prior's part and the corporation's for the rest of the town.[8] We have not found any references to the Prior's coroner after the Black Death of 1349, and in the Tripartite Indenture of 1355 it was agreed that the corporation's coroner should operate throughout the town.[9]

From 1294 until the Prior's loss of the Earl's half in 1336, his coroners had regularly appeared as official witnesses, after the bailiff, in deeds conveying Coventry properties, which implies that they were normally present at the Prior's fortnightly court,[10] but of their main functions we have no record except for sparse references in the rolls of the itinerant justices.[11] The Prior's coroners' own rolls which they compiled against the justices' visit have been lost, and our broken series of rolls begins in 1355 with that of John de Baldeswell,[12] the first corporation coroner to operate throughout the whole city. His jurisdiction was not confined to the town; he is described as 'coroner of the liberty of the town of Coventry', and he operated in the surrounding villages included in the manor of Cheylesmore. Though chosen by the corporation, he represented the King's authority, and by the mid- fourteenth century his regular duties had become settled as:-

(1) holding inquests on people who died by violence or accident
(2) hearing 'appeals' (that is, accusations by individuals) of felonies,especially appeals by 'approvers' - criminals who turned king's evidence to save their own necks, and
(3) seeing that felons who had taken sanctuary in churches were prevented from escaping, and eventually abjured the realm.[13]

After 1378 he also supervised the swearing in of the mayor at the beginning of his year of office, so saving him the journey to Westminster to take the oath in the Exchequer.[14]

Except for rare cases of treasure trove, the modern coroner is concerned with the investigation of all deaths which are not obviously natural, and already by the fourteenth century that had become his main function. The incomplete series of Coventry coroners' rolls record their actions on 105 occasions from 1354 to the end of the century; 89 were inquests on people 'found dead', and it is illuminating that, while 41 were killed in 38 accidents, more, 44, died by homicide. Eight were found to have died naturally.[15] John the servant of John Fletcher, who drowned himself in Swanswell Pool, was the only suicide recorded,[16] though it is possible that some of the deaths returned as accidental drownings could have been suicides.[17]

In view of the time which may elapse, and the massive amount of police work involved at the present day before a murder suspect is identified, it seems at first surprising that normally in fourteenth century Coventry a verdict naming the killer could be delivered in about 24 hours. Out of 42 cases of homicide, there were only two where the assailants were unknown, and both were in the outlying villages,[18] not in the town itself. But we must remember that these were not sophisticated crimes but mostly impulsive acts of violence, stabbings, blows with staves or whatever came handy, axes, stones, a spade or a hammer. A few were brutal murders in furtherance of robberies. Moreover, the jurors were not strangers weighing up the evidence, but fellow townsmen telling what they knew under the coroner's questioning. When Robert Seulere, 'Braban' (that is, Brabanter), killed Margaret le Longe, another Brabanter, one Gerekyn Braban, was on the jury.[19] John Fletcher was one of those returning a verdict of suicide on his servant John,[20] and Robert Glover was a juror when John Glover fell down a well.[21] After the death of a baby through accidental burns, his father was included in the jury.[22] In a small community the jurors may well have known something about the brawls which ended fatally, either at first hand or from others. Sometimes they were able to name accessories; two servants of John de Higham attacked Robert del Kechene with a knife and poleaxe and killed him, but the jurors named three more of Higham's employees, two servants of Robert de Waleshale and Master John le Flesshewer as being present and involved. Higham himself was not present, but received the others knowing what they had done. Flesshewer and Higham gave themselves up, but the rest of the gang fled. Robert was killed on Thursday night, his body found the next day, and the inquest followed on Saturday.[23]

A murder and a robbery at the Priory was described in some detail by the jurors; 'Geoffrey Wytles, at Coventry, by night feloniously, within Coventry Priory, in a house called the Sacrist's *(sexterii)*, where John, William and Ralph dwelt, outrageously *(enormiter)* struck them on their heads with an axe worth twopence, and feloniously killed and traitorously murdered them and bore away 40 marks in money and divers treasures *(jocalibus)* worth £10.'[24] At the least the jury identified the weapon and the position of the wound: the assailant 'feloniously struck the said John with a club under the right ear', or 'with a knife below the left rib'.[25]

It was, of course, very desirable to give a full account of the circumstances where a man killed another in self-defence, and the jury's verdict on the death of Hugh de Wenlok not only provides a graphic picture of the events of the night of May 31st 1357, but gives us a rare glimpse of the Coventry keepers of the peace in action. Hugh attempted to rob the house of a widow, Isabel de Lancastre, by breaking through the wall, but when he had got only halfway through Isabel sprang out of bed, naked, hit him on the head with a staff and raised the hue and cry, first from within the house and then outside. This brought the keepers of the peace to the spot, and with ,them William atte Hoo carrying a lighted candle. Hugh climbed on a pile of wood and hid himself under a coffer, but was discovered by William and others who called on him to surrender to the peace. Instead he attacked William with a knife. In self-defence William took a knife from the hand of a stranger, and stabbed Hugh to the heart. He then gave himself up and was lodged in gaol in the custody of the bailiffs.[26] Normally he would get the king's pardon, but not until he had been before the justices of gaol delivery.

The naming of a killer by the jurors was only the first step in a process which might eventually end in execution. Mostly the inquests reported that the accused had fled, so the first problem was to find and imprison him. But did others get away with undetected murders? Coroners' inquests were only held when there was a body to be seen. In an urban area it was not an easy matter to dispose of a corpse secretly, but murderers sometimes tried to evade detection by dumping their victims far from the place where they died. In the Coventry coroners' rolls we have only one unidentified body, found in Caludon.[27] He can hardly have been a villager, and if he belonged to the town, surely someone would have identified him. Was he a traveller, robbed and left dead on the Leicester road, or was he the victim of a crime committed outside the Liberty of Coventry?

'Henry Whelewright of Astley, with a staff worth a penny, feloniously struck the said Elias on the head'; 'John de Ashford feloniously struck John de Pole below his left rib with a knife worth eightpence';[28] these bizarre juxtapositions in juries' verdicts of a tragic blow and the mundane valuation of the weapon remind us that a coroner's inquest was concerned not only with the cause of death, but also with the pickings which would accrue to the royal exchequer. The original appointment of keepers of the pleas of the crown in 1194 was motivated by the desire for better justice, but also by Richard I's pressing need for money: the forfeitures due to the king when a man was hanged must not be neglected.[29] The king was entitled to any weapon used in murder or manslaughter (or its value). He also took the goods and chattels not only of convicted felons but of anyone who fled after a death, even if they were eventually found to be innocent. A felon's freehold land went to his immediate lord, but only after the king had 'year, day and waste', that is, possession of the land for a year and a day, with the right to demolish buildings, fell trees, plough up grassland and generally take what short-term gains he could. In practice he might get a money payment from the lord in lieu of his rights. It is said that few felons had land,[30] but Richard de Merston, who was hanged about 1327, had a messuage in Cross Cheaping. The Prior took the messuage as Richard's lord, ignoring the king's rights, and it was eight years before the matter came to light.[31]

But in 1344 Edward granted his right to felons' and fugitives' goods and to 'year, day and waste' of felons' lands, within the bounds of the Cheylesmore view of frankpledge (provided the criminals or fugitives were tenants or residents there) to his mother, Queen Isabella, for life. Once the new corporation was established, Isabella transferred her rights to it as part of the packet of privileges for which the corporation was to pay her £50 a year. The Black Prince, as Isabella's successor in Coventry, confirmed the grant for himself and his heirs, thus ensuring that for the indefinite future the chattels and the wasting of the lands belonged to the corporation.[32]

They derived no great profit from them: in the surviving coroners' rolls, nothing is said about any of the suspects having lands or houses, and if we took the verdicts at their face value we should have to conclude that homicides were mostly committed by the destitute, as two thirds of those accused were said to have no goods or chattels.[33] But we must regard these verdicts with some suspicion. It seems unlikely that John de Northampton, one of a family of butchers, who had at least one employee, and who killed in self-defence,[34] had nothing, or that two men who killed their wives[35] had no household goods. Juries are said to have undervalued felons' chattels, sometimes at the prompting of coroners who kept the difference for themselves.[36] It also seems likely that steps were taken by an accused man's family or friends to conceal or remove his possessions, or claim that they belonged to a relative, but we have no evidence to prove this. Perhaps some coroners were more conscientious than others; none of the killers named in Robert de Bruggeford's roll seemingly owned anything.[37]

Where chattels were recorded the jurors usually just gave a value ranging from twopence for the goods of a carter[38] to £20 for John le Parchmyners.[39] If he was really a parchment-maker he must have held a considerable stock. In only three cases did the jurors say what the items valued were: the butcher William Caumbrugge had a horse worth 6s 8d at Pinley;[40] William Nedler had two *lintheamina* and one *tapetum*.[41] These are general terms covering a variety of linen articles and hangings or carpets - they could have been two sheets and a rug for his bed, but there are other possibilities. Exceptionally, in the case of William Bythebrok of Foleshill, who killed a man in self-defence but then fled, we are given a detailed inventory of the possessions of a small farmer. His kitchen, dairy and brewing equipment including eleven vessels of wood or earthenware variously named, a trestle table and two gallons of linseed in a 'mashfat' were worth 8s 4d. His 'lead', perhaps a fixed vessel with provision for a fire underneath, appraised separately, at four shillings, was the most valuable item in his house. His furniture was a screen, a metebord (? a table for his meals), and a chair, four forms and a stool, valued together at three shillings. His cooking vessels were a brass pot and three bowls or pans worth 3s 4d. His 'wealth' was in his farm stock: two cows and four pigs at 25s were worth more than all the contents of his house.

No doubt one of the pig's predecessors had provided the eight pennyworth of 'bacon and grease'. A foal or colt was priced at 2s 6d. The inventory was taken in November, so there was hay and corn from the summer's harvest, worth five shillings. A bunch *(remule)* and a half of flax worth 18 pence and two shillingsworth of old iron brought the total value of his chattels to 55s 4d.[42] Apart from John le Parchmyner's, only two valuations exceeded this: Richard Andrew, who stabbed the girdler William Cryspe, had possessions worth 65s,[43] and John Hay, the parson of Bedworth and John his son or servant, accessories to the murder of the keeper of Cheylesmore Park, had £100 worth between them,[44] but Bedworth was not within the Cheylesmore leet, so the corporation would not get the Hays' goods. Their right to any of the goods was not established by the verdict of the coroner's jury; only after trial and conviction in a higher court could the corporation take possession, and conviction was by no means certain. Meanwhile the goods must be kept safely, and it is illustrative of the complications of jurisdictions in the Liberty of Coventry that while the town coroner took inquests throughout the Liberty, it was only within the town itself that the bailiffs were responsible for safe custody.[45] The lord of Pinley was responsible for William Caumbrugge's horse,[46] while the parker of Cheylesmore manor 'arrested' William Bythebrok's goods and animals on behalf of Sir Baldwyn de Beresford, to whom Richard II had granted the manor of Cheylesmore for life.[47]

Forty-one died by 'misfortune' *(infortuna)*, or, as we would say, by accident or misadventure. Accidents reflect the way people live and work, so what hazards did the Coventrians face in an age without mechanical transport, and when corn and fulling mills turned by wind and water were the only power-driven machinery? We have no record of non-fatal injuries, but of the 41 deaths investigated by the coroners, 20 were drownings. Rivers are dangerous in any age, and the Sherbourne (now mostly invisible in culverts), and the Sowe claimed five victims, including Katherine Scarlet who fell off her stilts into the water.[48] Others drowned in a pond and ditch, and a child fell into water at the end of a curtilage,[49] but the greatest hazard was drawing water from wells. Even Jordan Well, provided for the city by the wealthy wool merchant and mayor, Jordan de Shepey, was not completely safe, for Henry Cartere's daughter Alice fell in and was drowned.[50] Nearby, in Gosford Street, Joan

Mid 19th Century illustration of Well Street, Coventry.
Showing surviving part of Coventry city wall from a sketch by Dr Nathaniel
Troughton. The Troughton Collection includes 10 volumes of pencil
drawings of Coventry street scenes, buildings and interiors, plus some 18th
and 19th century prints. Troughton, a surgeon, was born in 1794 and died
in 1868. PA1/2/33b. *Reproduced courtesy of Coventry Archives.*

Appulton fell into Robert Blatherwyke's well. Her father's servant in trying to help her, fell in himself, as did another man who heard their cries, and all three drowned. The coroner ordered Blatherwyke's well to be filled in with stones and earth,[51] but not Jordan Well, nor apparently three others in which people died.[52] Three people drowned in 'pits' which could have been flooded quarry holes, rainwater reservoirs or almost any holes full of water. Again, only one was filled in.[53] Latrines were another medieval hazard,[54] and John de Maxstoke's servant Cecilia drowned in one.[55]

Burnings and scaldings in the house caused the deaths of six people; children were left lying close to open fires, and six-months old William Strynger, while his guardian's wife was out getting milk for him, touched a burning log so that the fire fell from the hearth and fatally burned him,[56] and John le Smyth's son died from the fire igniting his cradle during the night.[57] Grout, a kind of porridge made with coarse meal, was prepared in large containers, and a woman and boy were scalded to death through falling into them, while John Geffray's daughter Joan, fell into a masshefat of hot water.[58] Candles on walls were an obvious risk. One fell off and set a woman's bed on fire,[59] while Agnes Scryvein died, not by fire, but through standing on a stool to cut down her wall candle, when she fell off on to the stand for a yarn winder *(zarewyndelfoot)* and died two hours later.[60] Another fall, from a stair resulted in a broken neck for Agnes Croppill.[61]

It is perhaps worth mentioning that there are no inquests on people burned to death or suffocated through their houses catching fire. Perhaps, although thatched, timber-framed houses were obviously inflammable, it was comparatively easy to escape from them. Five men died in accidents with horses and carts: one was kicked, another fell under a cart wheel.[62] Two others were killed when their carts 'fell on' them, which presumably means they tipped over; in one case the cart was loaded with timber. Timber-transporting was obviously a dangerous business, for a fifth victim was killed when a piece of timber drawn by a mare fell on him.[63] Surprisingly, there are no cases of accidental deaths of riders of saddle horses. Apart from the carters, there are only two records of fatal accidents at work: a carpenter fell from his ladder,[64] and two men were buried while excavating sand and gravel on Hearsall Common for the surfacing of Spon Street.[65] There was one archery accident. John Reson, practising on a Sunday shooting at targets, hit John Stafford in the chest.[66]

Whatever the other hazards, there is always the weather ! On September 23rd 1357 Joan de Coleshull died in a snow and hail storm while pasturing her sheep at Foleshill.[67] Robert de Roucestre was blown by a gust of wind and fell on to a piece of timber at the bottom of Earl's Mill floodgates[68] and a boy playing in the road at Whitley was killed by a falling branch.[69]

Coroners were expected to hold inquests on everyone who died in prison, and to inquire whether the death was due to torture or harsh treatment. Only two such inquests appear on the Coventry rolls. One man was found to have died from plague,[70] but in the case of Richard Brodook who had obvious injuries a longer explanation was elicited. Brodook was suspected of being one of a particularly brutal gang of robbers who, having robbed two brothers and killed one of them, kept the other bound hand and foot to the corpse for two days and nights. The surviving brother, John Hosier of Tring in Hertfordshire, accused Brodook before the Coventry Bailiffs who had him arrested and gaoled 'until the truth be better known'. A month later he died. The jurors found that immediately on his commission to prison he had been put in leg-irons, and that night made a determined attempt to break out of them but merely inflicted injuries on his shins and ankles from which he eventually died.[71] It would, of course, not be surprising for wounds to turn septic in medieval gaols.

The royal exchequer profited from accidental deaths. Animals or objects which caused death were forfeit as 'deodands'. The word means 'to be given to God', that is, the Church, for the benefit of the poor, but it had long been the custom that the king had them. So the jurors had to value them: a halfpenny for the fallen branch, a penny for the arrow, a shilling for the grout, 40 pence for the horse which kicked,[72] and so on. Wells could cause complications if they were found to be the cause of death, but this was usually avoided in Coventry by blaming the windlasses, valued at two to three shillings.[73] Local juries protected the owners of offending objects by undervaluing them or by limiting the definition of deodands, for example the cartwheel only was forfeited not the cart.[74] But in 1397 local jurisdictions were suspended while the Court of King's Bench was sitting in Coventry, and when the King's Bench coroner held the inquest on the man killed by a cart loaded with timber the jurors had to value the wood (eighteen pence), the cart (13s 4d) and one horse (7s), but not the other horses in the team as they were not moving, the rule being that 'all things which move to the death are deodands'. The total of (£1 1s 10d) was more than three times the highest valuation (6s for a cart) at inquests held by the Coventry coroners. In the charters whereby the forfeited goods of felons and fugitives are given to the corporation there is no mention of deodands,[75] so presumably they continued to go to the Exchequer, though the procedures for ensuring that they did were not.[76] Within the town, the bailiffs were responsible for them; elsewhere in the liberty the townships took charge.[77]

The coroner would only hold inquests on people who died naturally if death was sudden or unexpected; if the body was found in the open and the cause of death was unknown; if there was the possibility or suspicion that death was not natural; or if it occurred in gaol. So in the surviving coroners' rolls we have only eight natural deaths, four from plague,[78] one from abscesses (*postim 'impostumes'*[79]) and the remaining three from ill fortune or infirmity and the will of God.[80]

It was part of the coroner's duties to act on appeals of felony. Appeal, a formal accusation, a kind of private prosecution, made by an individual, had once been the commonest procedure for bringing criminals before the courts, but by the fourteenth century it had been largely superseded by the indictments of the coroners' and other presenting juries. However, it was still used occasionally, for instance in 1357 when the Coventry coroner's jury returned a verdict that John le Parchmyner had fatally stabbed William Daventry (and an indictment presumably followed automatically) the dead man's widow appealed Parchmyner before the coroner.[81] A woman could go to the coroner to appeal a man of rape, and we know of one such case in Coventry.[82] Six other appeals by injured parties alleged some kind of theft or robbery.[83] As there was no corpse to be viewed, the coroner did not assemble a jury but himself initiated the process which led to trial, as when John

Clifton of Northampton appealed the smith Richard de Halughton of robbing him at Coombe wood, of a black horse with saddle and bridle, his bag, hood, hose, and £14 in money, Richard was lodged in gaol to await the justices of gaol delivery.[84] As they did not like appeals, which could end in trial by battle, the king's justices insisted on strict procedures which made the process difficult to complete. Whether for this reason, or because the appellors found other means of redress, two appeals of housebreaking were not pursued further, and Sir John Peyto of Chesterton in south Warwickshire, who had come before the Coventry coroner to appeal Robert Rychemund of stealing two horses, then let the matter drop.[85] But the Coventry butcher, Robert Lirpol, successfully prosecuted a pair of nocturnal cattle-rustlers who had driven off twenty-two beasts which he had pastured in Earlsdon. They were tried by jury and sentenced to be hanged.[86]

As we have said, the ordinary appeal of felony, while not completely obsolete by the fourteenth century, was no longer the usual way of bringing criminals to trial, but was essential when a felon decided to turn 'approver', that is to try to save his own life by accusing his accomplices. In court or in gaol, rating his chances of acquittal as poor, he would plead guilty, confess his crimes, and ask for a coroner 'for the king's profit'. He then had to swear to appeal all his accomplices, and was given three days in which to do so to the coroner. The unedifying story of William de Bury, alias William del Chaumbre de Bury, illustrates the working of the system and depicts the kind of rogue who mingled on the roads with the merchants and pilgrims when Chaucer was young.

After a successful run of thefts over seven months in 1356, during which he travelled over five hundred miles Bury's luck ran out in Coventry. On market day, Friday October 1st he and three others stole from a Birmingham draper a cloak, three belts, a pair of hose, and seven ells of russet cloth. By October 29th the coroner, John de Baldeswell, was hearing Bury's confession in gaol which suggests that Bury was arrested soon after the theft and was perhaps 'taken with the mainour', that is actually carrying some of the stolen property. If so, his chances of avoiding hanging would be slim unless he turned approver, which he did admitting the theft and appealing three confederates, John Themelere of Weston, Margaret de Norton, and William Spicer of Uppingham. The coroner came again on Monday and Tuesday, and Bury made more confessions going back to March 25th when he and John atte More of Reading stole three horses which they sold later to an Oxford man. Three days later Bury was at Worcester market with a different partner, and they stole three brass pots. By May 3rd he was in Yorkshire where he and another man stole a pair of boots and three ells of red cloth. Heading south, he was involved in the theft of three dozen belts at Wetherby, housebreaking at Waltham Cross, and by August 24th was in London, where he and a confederate stole a silver pendant. Returning north, there were thefts at Baldock and Newmarket where a draper in the market was relieved of twelve ells of blue cloth by Bury, Robert Joye, a Staffordshire draper, and two others. And so to Coventry, detection, and gaol. Altogether Bury named fourteen confederates, but they were not an organised gang who travelled the country together. He seems to have formed temporary or ad hoc alliances, and then moved on to find new partners: none of those he appealed was involved in more than one theft, and Margaret Norton was the only woman.[87]

Merely appealing his companions in crime did not save an approver from hanging. Those he had appealed must be arrested - if they could be found - and he must then 'prove' his allegations, and proof often meant trial by battle. First Robert Joye, Bury's accomplice at Newmarket, was caught and jailed and on May 8th 1358 they faced each other before the justices of gaol delivery. Joye chose battle: he would defend himself 'by his right hand as an honest men against a felon', while Bury undertook to prove his case 'as a felon against a felon'. Joye was defeated and sentenced to be hanged, while Bury was returned to prison.[88] Two years later he faced another accomplice: a John de Harley, arrested for an offence not connected with Bury, turned out to be the John atte More who, Bury said, helped him to steal horses at Salisbury. Before the justices, he denied the accusations, and undertook to prove his innocence by battle, which was fixed for the hour of vespers, on April 16th in the New Park at Coventry. It was the end of the road for Bury. Although he had agreed to fight, when it came to the point he defaulted, saying he did not know how to defend his appeal against More. Inevitably he was ordered to be hanged.[89] It may seem surprising that he should surrender to his fate without a fight, but these battles were fought with savage ferocity, and faced with an opponent certain to overwhelm him, a man might opt for being hanged straight away rather than being battered into impotence and hanged afterwards. By turning approver Bury had probably delayed his execution by three and a half years. Medieval gaols were not very secure, and it is said that criminals turned approver to gain a respite during which they hoped to escape. If that was Bury's aim, Coventry gaol defeated him, though it was possible to escape from it.[90]

None of the other approvers we know of who confessed to the Coventry coroners admitted such a catalogue of thefts or had travelled so widely as Bury, nor did they accuse so many accomplices. Roger de Chersale admitted only stealing nine nobles from Sir William Ryvel at Henley near Coventry and sharing them with Thomas Randolf of Foleshill;[91] John Cartere and his accomplice had stolen a horse at Foleshill, and two books worth 20s and a towel at Rugby, and although the coroner conscientiously visited Cartere on the two days following his confession, he had nothing more to add.[92] The Welshman, William Gogh, had more to tell. In two confessions made in July and November 1376, he admitted thefts going back to 1370, but unlike Bury, he was not a general 'snapper up of unconsidered trifles'. He only stole horses and cattle. Apart from the theft of five cows from Sowe, Gogh operated in Leicestershire and Northamptonshire, but brought his booty back to Coventry. The horses he stole at East Farndon, Normanton, and near Whitwick, could, of course be ridden, but the ten oxen and cows from Welford must have been driven over twenty miles without effective pursuit or challenge.

Gogh appealed seven accomplices, one a pardoner, John Taillour, who was arrested and opted for trial by jury. Another, Hugh de Barwe, was a butcher. According to Gogh, Barwe had helped him to steal the five cows from Sowe, and had slaughtered them in Coventry. And when two of Gogh's accomplices had arrived in Coventry with the ten beasts from Welford, Barwe, knowing of the theft, had received the rustlers and cattle near Swanswell Pool.[93] Butchers were obvious suspects for complicity in cattle stealing as well as victims of it. We have seen that Robert Lirpol secured a sentence of hanging against two men who had stolen his cattle, but ten years earlier he had been appealed by an approver, William Spencer, of Wendlebury in Oxfordshire, as one of his companions in a theft of cattle in Leicestershire. Lirpol chose trial by battle and on July 22nd 1384 at Coventry he overcame his accuser who was sentenced to be hanged.[94]

In October 1356 a coroner's jury inquiring into the death in Ironmonger Row of the ironmonger William de Sutton, found that he had been attacked at Guphill Ford on the western outskirts of Coventry by John Pecok and John de Roseleye. Armed with a sword and knife they had robbed him of two horses and the forty ploughshares they were carrying and given him a headwound from which he died six days later. Before they could be arrested the killers took sanctuary in the Priory bell-tower, where they were entitled to remain under the protection of the Church for forty days, after which they could avoid execution by 'abjuring the realm' - taking a solemn oath to leave the kingdom forever. The coroner was the essential official in the procedure: he visited the two in the Priory, and the right to abjure could only be granted if they confessed a felony to him. They did not admit the robbery and murder of Sutton, but Pecok confessed to killing a man at Barnet in Hertfordshire two years before, and Roseleye to an even earlier killing at Bodmin in Cornwall. For some reason Pecok relinquished his right to sanctuary and asked to be put in Coventry gaol. Possibly he was a clerk and exempt from the death penalty, or he might have taken steps to purchase a pardon. Roseleye remained in the bell-tower for forty days and then, before the coroner, solemnly abjured the realm of England. He was given Southampton as his port of embarkation, and 'took the cross', that is, was given a wooden cross to carry showing he was under the protection of the Church.[95] By the mid-fourteenth century he was no longer required to wear a special garment of sackcloth, but he should have been bare-headed and without stockings. The coroner had to set him on the highway and admonish him to go straight to Southampton by the most direct route.[96]

Any consecrated church, chapel or monastery with its burial ground provided sanctuary, and in addition to the church of St Mary's Priory, fugitives took refuge in the chapel of St John's Hospital, the guild chapel in Bablake,[97] and, in the case of Roger de

Allerton who had managed to escape from Coventry gaol, St Michael's. Allerton was from Northallerton, and in company with his fellow Yorkshireman, John de Awene of Beverley, had stolen a horse with saddle and bridle, money, and five pounds worth of bed hangings. Awene was a clerk and was put in the bishop's prison, but Allerton, in St Michael's churchyard before the coroner, abjured the realm and was set on his way to Chester,[98] which was a port for Ireland where sanctuary men could legally go as they only abjured the realm of England. So for Peter Corrat of Ireland, who fled to Bablake chapel and was given Liverpool as his port,[99] abjuration was merely going home. Corrat and three others who found sanctuaries in Coventry while William de Attleburgh was coroner, were all said to have done so for fear of their enemies.[100] Perhaps this was a standard formula of Attleburgh or his clerk, but often a man was more immediately in danger from seekers after private vengeance than from the bailiffs and constables aiming merely to arrest him. But once in a sanctuary, a fugitive could not abjure and travel under the protection of the Church unless he confessed a felony. So some confessions were inventions.[101] Peter Corrat admitted homicide and the theft of a widow's horse; the brothers Nicholas and Thomas Sprot, homicide, Thomas Lovecock of Grendon the theft of a coverlet worth 3s,[102] but we have no way of knowing whether their confessions were true.

Whatever their reasons, sanctuary seekers were a nuisance and a burden to the neighbourhood which was reponsible for seeing that, once in church, the fugitives stayed there until their formal abjuration. The coroner charged the town's bailiffs to see that watch was kept day and night for forty days, and in the case of Peter Corrat recorded that the neighbours at once surrounded him.[103] This duty would not be such a burden in a populous town as in a small village whose church sheltered a fugitive, but nevertheless the Coventrians would be glad to see the felon take the road to his port.

But did he actually reach it? The tanner William Tasker never did, nor intended to. He was a Coventry man, but after stealing and selling a brass pan and various items of clothing and bedding, took refuge in the church at Kineton in south Warwickshire, where he abjured before a county coroner. But within weeks he was reported to have 'returned' and to be wandering the country. If any attempts were made to arrest him they were unsuccessful and he was eventually outlawed.[104] Although 'returning' abjurors and even those who strayed from the direct route to the port could be arrested and hanged or even summarily beheaded, most, like Tasker, were prepared to take the risk, and only a small minority ever went overseas.[105]

The broken series of Coventry coroners' rolls covers just under a third of the years from 1355 to 1399.[106] Eighty-five people are accused in them as principals, accomplices, harbourers, or receivers of stolen property. Not all were guilty, many were never tried, and some, named as accomplices in crimes committed in far-off places by approvers or abjurors, probably never came to Coventry. But one fact calls for comment; this assorted company of alleged felons included only one woman, Margaret Norton, appealed by William de Bury as one of his accomplices in a theft of cloth at Coventry.[107] But when we turn to the contemporaneous rolls of the justices of the peace in Coventry between 1377 and 1397, we find many offences by women, nineteen of them felonious.[108] One incident which should certainly have been on the coroner's roll was the killing of a weaver by two men and their wives in 1376,[109] but that year's roll is missing. Apart from this and two cases of receiving felons (one another woman), the women's alleged offences were all thefts: of yarn, wool, clothing, bed-linen, rosaries, silver, and in one case, money.[110] It seems to have become the practice to have these offences presented by the jurors or constables at the quarterly sessions of the J.P.s in preference to appeals by individual victims of theft before the coroner. While women were involved in assaults, sometimes on other women, only the one just mentioned ended fatally and became a felony. Horse stealing, cattle rustling and highway robbery were male preserves, and no approver or abjuror except William de Bury named a woman accomplice. We now turn from the malefactors to those responsible for investigating their crimes and formally accusing them.

Showing detail of a cattle auction at market c.1500.
MS. Gough liturg.7, fol.10. Calendar, Flemish, C1500.
Reproduced courtesy of the Bodleian Library, University of Oxford.

Showing detail of Friars, 2nd quarter 13th Century.
MS. Douce 180, p.35. Apocalypse, English, 2nd quarter 13th Century.
Reproduced courtesy of the Bodleian Library, University of Oxford.

Chapter 2: The Prior's Coroner

Originally, coroners were elected in the county courts, but when lords of liberties obtained the privilege of having their own coroner, as the Prior did in 1267, they usually appointed him themselves.[1] The priors in the late thirteenth century chose their coroners from the same group of servitors which provided their bailiffs. It would seem that by 1280 the Prior had managed to establish a single court for the two halves of the town, where his bailiff presided. The coroner was normally present, and appears as witness after the bailiff on deeds acknowledged in court. Their regular attendance at what must often have been mere routine sessions of the court suggests that the Prior's coroners were concerned with business not strictly part of their duties as keepers of the pleas of the Crown. By the reign of Edward II the system was well established and working smoothly, as evidenced by the long tenures of office of the bailiff John de Clifton (fifteen years), and the coroner Roger de Pacwode (thirty years).[2] The events of the first twenty years of Edward III's reign, however, diminished both offices: with Isabella's resumption of the Earl's-half lordship followed by the changes to the boundaries of the two halves, the Prior's bailiff's authority was restricted to a mere remnant of the old Prior's half, and in 1346 the grant to the new corporation of a coroner of their own confined the Prior's coroner to the same area.[3] Obviously there was less work to do, and the last Prior's coroner, William le Palmer, was simultaneously bailiff.[4] Finally, by the Tripartite Indenture of 1355 the Prior relinquished his rights, and the corporation's coroner functioned throughout the city and suburbs.[5]

The original instructions in 1194 ordered that a team of three knights and a clerk should be coroners in each county, but by the fourteenth century most coroners were not knights, and the stipulation that one coroner should be a clerk was very quickly dropped. In fact it has been authoritatively stated that only two medieval coroners, one for Ipswich and the other for Grimsby, are known to have been clerks.[6] But of the six Prior's coroners who held office between 1307 and 1355, three, Anketin de Colleshull, Roger de Pacwode, and Roger Oky were clerks, while Simon Pakeman was a professional lawyer.[7] Henry le Baxtere, apparently, was neither a clerk nor a lawyer, but came from a family which served the Prior for three generations, for his father and grandfather had both been bailiffs, and was possibly a merchant.[8] So was William Palmer, the last Prior's coroner. It was to be men of this type, rather than administrators and lawyers, who held the position of the corporation's coroner.

Table 1: The Prior's Coroners:

reigns of Edward II and Edward III[*]

	First reference as coroner	Last reference as coroner
Anketin de Coleshull clerk	26 Feb 1307[9]	19 Apr 1309[10]
Roger de Pacwode, clerk	18 Feb 1310[11]	7 Nov 1340[12]
Henry le Baxtere	2 Mar 1341[13]	25 Apr 1342[14]
Simon Pakeman	28 Jul 1342[15]	24 May 1344[16]
Roger Oky clerk	22 Sep 1344[17]	25 Feb 1345[18]
William le Palmer	25 Apr 1345[19]	13 May 1349[20]

*For earlier coroners, see Coss, *Early Records*, xxix

Appendix

Simon Pakeham

Five of the six fourteenth-century Prior's coroners came from established Coventry families, whose surnames appear in documents of the previous century. But Simon Pakeman was obviously a newcomer, who by 1310 had acquired a house in the

Pottersrow, close to both the Priory and the market, which was to be his main residence and which by 1334 included two shops.[21] He was married by 1322 when he and Agnes his wife conveyed a messuage, part of her inheritance, to Thomas Waleys. Perhaps there was some dispute over this transaction, as later in the year Pakeman, with thirteen men and two women, was accused of assaulting Waleys and breaking his arms.[22]

In 1322 when Edward II was collecting men at Coventry to deal with Thomas of Lancaster's rebellion, the Coventrians granted the king £100, plus the expenses of a hundred armed men for forty days. The money was raised by a levy on about 280 citizens who paid varying amounts, presumably according to their wealth. Pakeman paid five shillings, more than most contributors, but a substantial minority paid more, and while obviously a man of substance, Pakeman was not in the same class as the Huntes, three of whom paid £3 or more, Laurence de Shepeye (£6 13s 4d) or Hugh de Merington (£10).[23] In 1327 and 1332 parliament granted a subsidy, a tax on those able to pay, based on a fraction of their movable goods, a twentieth in 1327, and for Coventrians, a fifteenth in 1332. With some exceptions, individuals' contributions were lower than their payments in 1322. But Pakeman's shilling in the Prior's part on both occasions puts him among the very lowest taxpayers: only one other man in Coventry paid so little in 1332, and a mere six people paid a penny or two less in 1327. However, he paid another sixteen pence in Coundon in 1327, but not in 1332.[24] It could be that there had been a decline in his fortunes, but more likely the method of assessment in 1322, which is not known, was to his disadvantage.

Other evidence suggests that in fact Pakeman prospered: another messuage was conveyed to him in 1311, and in 1326 he and Agnes acquired land in Whoberley.[25] In August 1335 he and his son Guy had a lease for lives from the Priory of a considerable property at the far end of Spon Street, beyond the bridge, which included a cottage at the gate, a dovecote, field, croft, 14 selions of arable land and a piece of meadow. The rent was to be 26 shillings and eightpence a year.[26] Agnes was not mentioned in the lease, and had probably died shortly before, as the executors of her will had completed their duties by October 1337.[27] This property in Spon

End was close to Whoberley where Pakeman had added to the land he and Agnes acquired in 1326, so he now had a considerable holding on the western fringe of the city. It is unlikely that he farmed it himself, and in 1341 he leased out the Whoberley lands for a sixteen year term with option to renew.[28]

Little has come to light about professional or public activities during his early years in Coventry. He first appears in 1324 in a list of over a hundred men who become sureties for the payment of the fines amounting to 800 marks (£533) imposed on the Warwickshire assessors and collectors of the subsidies.[29] From 1327 he appears frequently as a witness to deeds including those where the Priory's agent, William de Passenham, acquired property on the monks' behalf. On several occasions he is the last witness,[30] and the authentication by his seal of two grants to Passenham where Pakeman was neither a party nor a witness is further evidence that he was engaged in conveyancing business for the Priory.[31] But his legal practice was not confined to Coventry: in 1336 and 1337 he was practicing as an attorney in the Court of Common Pleas, at that time located in York because of the war with Scotland. One of his clients was the abbot of St Evroult in Normandy who was suing the Prioress of Nuneaton for arrears of rent; another was the earl of Warwick, Thomas Beauchamp.[32]

By May 1339, Pakeman had become the Prior's bailiff.[33] His authority would normally be exercised in the much reduced Prior's half, but the Prior owned properties, let to tenants, in the Earl's half, and when Pakeman went to collect the rents he was assaulted by a gang led by Peter de Stoke.[34] But his authority as coroner from July 1342 to 1344 extended over the whole city, and he obviously attended the Earl's-half court and witnessed deeds after the Earl's-half bailiff.[35] He had given up his office by late September 1344, but his professional career was not yet at an end: trouble had broken out in Coventry between William Walshman, the controller of the New Drapery in Earl Street, and William Waldive of Alspath, whose supporters included Peter de Stoke and other well-known Coventrians. Early in 1345 both men petitioned the king, alleging assaults and requesting an enquiry and the trial of their opponents. Walshman got in first, and as he was Queen Isabella's servant it was she who sent his petition to her son. Relying, no doubt, on the queen's influence, Walshman asked to be excused the usual fee for a writ appointing justices to hear and determine the case. He also added the names of the justices he would like, including two of the royal judges and Pakeman. The writ was duly issued[36] and later in the year Pakeman was appointed one of the justices to deal with a more serious matter, the violent death of the abbot of Coombe, but after three weeks he and his colleagues were told not to proceed.[37]

Perhaps Pakeman died soon afterwards as there are no further references to him, and the house and shops in Ironmonger Row (or Potters' Row) and the arable in Whoberley were in other hands by 1352.[38] He had, however, a younger, more eminent namesake who may well have been a relative, though the connection has not been traced. This Simon was of Kirkby Mallory, Leicestershire, but he had links with Coventry families: in 1350 a considerable estate in North Warwickshire held by the wealthy Coventry merchant John Prest and his wife, was entailed on a boy, Simon le Couper, son of another Coventrian who held lands in Whoberley. In the event of failure of the direct line of descent from Couper, the estate was to go to 'Simon Pakeman of Kerby' and his heirs.[39]

Roger de Pacwode

Pakeman is the only Prior's coroner recorded in all three lists of Coventry taxpayers from 1322 to 1332. The only other coroner to contribute to any subsidy was Roger de Pacwode, who paid two shillings, twice as much as Pakeman, in the Prior's half in 1327.[40] Pacwode, a clerk,[41] was one of those appointed to collect the levy granted by the Coventrians in 1322, but apparently did not contribute himself, unless his name was one of the few on the list which cannot now be read.[42] The Pacwodes were established in Coventry before 1280,[43] and when Roger finally relinquished his office in the clean sweep of officials ordered by Edward III and his Council early in 1341, he had been coroner for over thirty years,[44] far longer than anyone else in the fourteenth century. But we know very little about him. He had a tenement in Marshall Lane (otherwise Palmer Lane) just round the corner from Pakeman's house, another property in Spon Street, and in 1334-5 was paying the Priory four shillings a year for two tenements in Much Park Street.[45] Possible relatives are two other clerks: Hugh de Pacwode who was a Priory agent in 1349-50 and later entered the service of Queen Philippa,[46] wife of Edward III, and Roger de Pacwode, King's clerk, who was granted a prebend in St Mary's Warwick in 1325.[47]

Before he became coroner Roger was the last witness to several deeds which he had probably written or drafted,[48] and in May 1306 he was one of the presenting jury who informed the king's justices of the violent deaths in Coventry during the previous nine years. (One of the murderers was William de Pacwode, tailor).

Anketin de Coleshull

Also on the jury in 1306 was Pacwode's predecessor as coroner, Anketin de Coleshull, another clerk.[49] Like Pacwode he appears several times as the last witness to deeds,[50] including Roger de Montalt's remission of forty shillings of his annual rent due from the Priory in 1289.[51] It is very likely that Coleshull was employed by the monks to draw up this deed. He must by then have been an experienced conveyancer, for he appears as last witness and clerk in 1272.[52] He was bailiff from 1298 to 1300 and twice again after his term as coroner, the last spell being in 1318-19[53] when he must have been in his middle sixties at the least. He had property in the Burges, Well Street and St Nicholas Street[54] and drew a rent of 7 shillings and 9 pence from a tenement in Bayley Lane until he conveyed it to his son John in 1303.[55]

Roger Oky

The last clerk to be coroner in the fourteenth century, Roger Oky, died in late February or early March 1345,[56] leaving to his son a considerable estate: 6 messuages, 4 shops, 6 cottages, 2 crofts, a quarry and garden which in 1380 were said to be worth £13 a year. At that time the crofts contained eight tenters (wooden fences on which weavers stretched and dried their cloth). There were also 24 acres called Chilterns Leyes in Radford, plus a messuage leased to Robert and Isabel Muyre for 26 shillings $1\frac{1}{4}$ pence a year.[57] What proportion of his final estate he inherited and how much came from a successful professional career cannot now be determined, but his family was long established in Coventry where Thomas Oky was reeve of the Prior's part about 1240.[58] A later Thomas paid the subsidy in Radford and Coundon in 1327 and 1332.[59] The family's base seems to have been the Bishop Street-Well Street area and the adjoining territory of Radford, Coundon and Spon. Certainly Roger had a property in Bishop Street which he leased to a future mayor, Sewall de Bulkington, in 1328.[60] A corner tenement at the junction of Bishop Street and Well Street had Roger's property adjoining on both streets, while at the other end of Well Street he was neighbour to William Oky and his wife Edith. He had another holding round the corner on the road from Bishop's Bar to Hill Mill,[61] so it seems likely that Viel's quarry in this area was the one which Roger had when he died.

In 1330 Oky acquired from Richard and Emma le Seeler a tenement at the Broadgate end of Smithford Street, leasing it back to them for lives at a rose rent.[62] He may have raised cash for this deal by selling two rents of two shillings and two and sixpence a year to the Priory,[63] but, however that may be, he was obviously well enough off at that time to be able to forgo current income for future profit. Yet he did not pay anything to the subsidies of 1327 or 1332. Whatever the reason,[64] his escape from tax shows that we cannot use non-payment as proof of poverty.

In 1332 Oky acquired from an earlier coroner, Henry le Baxtere, the right to receive 12 shillings rent for life from the White Cellar, a well-known inn at the corner of Earl Street and Much Park Street, and three years later he added to his stake in that area a cottage and a plot of land with a malt kiln, near the inn, granting a new lease to the sitting tenant.[65] In 1340 he leased one of his Well Street properties to the Blaby family for three lives,[66] and in 1343 he renewed his own lease of an enclave of arable in Radford, bounded on three sides by his own land.[67] Besides his tenement in Smithford Street he had another central property in Cross Cheaping.[68]

In 1342 he was involved in a bizarre case in the Court of Common Pleas: a messuage in Coventry, once William Oky's, had come into Roger's possession, and he had passed it to his son Henry. When William died, his widow Edith claimed a third of the property as her dower. Henry 'vouched' Roger to defend his title, thus making him a party in the case. Roger declared that Edith was not entitled to dower as William was still alive and living in Carlisle. Possibly he believed that, but more likely it was a ploy as he thought Edith would not be able to prove her husband's death. She declared that William had died when with Edward III's army in Antwerp in 1339. However, these were mere preliminary legal skirmishes; the case was adjourned to the next term for the parties to produce proof. On resumption, Edith produced two witness, one of them Roger le Hunte, described as of Ipswich, but almost certainly the wealthy Coventrian. They testified on oath that William had died in Ipswich on June 19th 1338, and that they had seen him buried there 'in St Laurence's churchyard on the south side of the church towards the east.' Not surprisingly, Henry and Roger were unable to resurrect William and Edith was awarded her dower.[69] Roger Oky was sometimes styled 'Master'.[70] As he was a clerk it could mean that he had a degree, but probably it was a recognition of his wealth and status in Coventry. But we have little evidence of his professional life. He often witnessed deeds, but only five have been found where he was the last witness. These occur between 1325 and 1330 and three of them concern the Priory or its agent William de Passenham.[71] His time as coroner was brief, from late September 1344 until his death five months later.[72] His heir was not Henry but another son, Roger, a hosier.[73]

Henry le Baxtere

Two of our six Prior's coroners were not clerks, and probably not lawyers, though we do not know what their occupations were. Henry le Baxtere was the third generation of his family to serve the Prior. His father Robert and his grandfather Henry had both been bailiffs.[74] Henry who became coroner is not styled bailiff in any document we have seen, but his appearance as first witness in several deeds relating to the remnant of the Prior's half from 1338 to 1342 suggests that he was presiding at the fortnightly court there, normally one of the bailiffs functions.[75] By March 1341 he had become coroner and was last mentioned in office on April 25th 1342.[76] We do not know how the Baxtere family built up their estate. Obviously an ancestor was a baker, but there is no evidence to suggest that the coroner ever was. However, by the time of his marriage, about 1332, to Agnes, the widow of William Basset, he had an unearned income of fifty shillings a year, which he arranged to have settled on himself and his wife jointly. The income came from rents ranging from ten shillings to sixpence, from properties in the Well Street - Bishop Street - St Nicholas Street area, held by tenants for life or years, which would of course eventually revert to Henry and Agnes or their heirs. But these were not their only expectations: Henry's widowed mother, another Agnes, had re-married and she and her husband, John de Hockleye, were Henry's tenants during their lives of unspecified lands and tenements in Keresley. Moreover, Hockleye had another holding in Bishop Street, which on his death was to go to Henry. These were quite apart from Agnes Hockleye's dower, her entitlement for life to a third of whatever real estate Robert le Baxtere had held while she was married to him. Her right was not affected by re-marriage and she and Hockleye held her share jointly: three shops in the market, plus a long tenement let out to the fishmongers, and annual rents amounting to fifty-five shillings and fourpence from ten properties, including more shops, cottages, a field and a capital messuage. All this dower would eventually come to Henry and his wife.[77] This marriage settlement, extensive as it was, does not give a complete picture of Baxtere's estate: he owned the White Cellar, and as we have seen, he conveyed a rent of twelve shillings a year to be taken from it to Roger Oky for life. Three years later he granted a rent for life from the same property to John de Meryngton.[78] Whether this was the rent originally settled on Oky which had been surrendered by him, or an extra charge on the White Cellar is not clear. Unless these rents were granted in exchange for property or as retainers, they must have been sold to raise money. They were not his only outgoings: in 1334-5 he was paying the Priory twenty four shillings annually for rent from divers messuages,[79] perhaps including those mentioned in the marriage settlement. But there were also other sources of income: in 1339 he leased his plot with pond in Angle Lane at ten shillings a year for sixty years, rising to thirty shillings thereafter.[80] The difference in the two rents suggests that he had sold the lease for a lump sum. In the next year he and Henry del Heth acquired a chief rent of twelve pence a year from a tenement in West Orchard.[81] More property came to Henry and Agnes from her family, the Bassets: a messuage in Hay Lane, another in Little Park Street, and four acres in the fields near the Millstones. There was also property in Wolvey, eight miles away to the north-east, which Agnes and William Basset held for their lives.[82]

By good fortune, documents have survived to give more information about Baxtere's property and income than we have for many of his contemporaries. It would be naive to think we have the full picture, but so far as it goes, it would appear that Baxtere and his wife were disposing of inherited property rather than adding to it: the messuage in Hay Lane was conveyed to Thomas de Coleshill in 1338, four acres of land went two years later, and in 1342 tenements in Broadgate and Cross Cheaping, and some Keresley property, probably that which Henry's mother and her second husband held for lives, went to Guy and Agnes Merington.[83] The date of the first deed in this last transaction was April 29th, four days after the last references to Baxtere as coroner.[84] On June 1st following he gave a chief rent of twelve pence from a property in West Orchard to John de Holand, Vicar of Holy Trinity, and a chaplain, John de Grendon. This was in effect a gift to the new guild of St John the Baptist, of which Holand was a founder, and Baxtere and his wife were almost certainly members.[85] It may have been a death-bed gift as there are no further references to Baxtere except as former owner of various properties.

Baxtere and his wife were certainly members of a guild, if not St John's then St Mary's or St Katherine's. This, taken together with Baxtere's prosecution of Jordan, son of Alexander Avery of Fillongley for an account of his receipts while receiver of money due to Baxtere[86] suggests membership of the mercantile community, foreshadowing the type of coroner who,would hold office under the corporation.

William Palmer

Baxtere is comparatively well-documented, but we know very little about the other non-clerical Prior's coroner, William Palmer. He was probably the last holder of the office, which he combined with that of bailiff in the reduced Prior's half. While originally he had jurisdiction as coroner throughout the city in 1346, the grant to the corporation of a coroner of their own restricted him to the small territory he administered as bailiff.[87] Palmer held land in Radford, and it was probably he who, in or before 1356, conveyed two curtilages there to an agent for eventual transfer to the Priory.[88] Eight years later, William Palmer, merchant, was mentioned as the previous owner of Palmer's Close in Radford, and a piece of arable near Hill Mill,[89] but it is uncertain whether this was the coroner or a namesake who was one of the Coventry bailiffs in 1379.

On Christmas Eve 1347, Palmer witnessed a deed relating to land opposite St Nicholas churchyard, presumably in the Prior's-half court. On the same day John de Arthingworth in the mayor's court witnessed a quitclaim of a meadow in Radford. Both witnessed as coroners,[90] but Palmer was the last of his kind, while Arthingworth was the first of a line of corporation coroners continuing for five centuries.

Chapter 3: The Corporation's Coroner

The switch from Prior's to corporation's coroners was, of course, one aspect of the victory of the mercantile community over the monks in the contest for control of the town. The coroner's basic function remained the same, though there were changes in the extra duties customarily performed by him outside his obligation to keep the pleas of the crown. He no longer appears regularly as one of the official witnesses to deeds, which implies that he was not expected to be present at the routine acknowledgements of them in the mayor and bailiffs' court. One would have assumed that he was present when criminals whose cases were sent for trial by the king's justices were indicted, but if so, in the early days, his presence was not recorded in the indictment: the rolls of the justices of gaol delivery say only that the malefactors had been indicted before the mayor and bailiffs.[1] Only from 1370 onwards is the coroner mentioned as well.[2] As we have seen, from 1378 he presided over the taking of the mayor's oath.[3] His jurisdiction now extended throughout the Liberty of Coventry, whereas the Prior's coroner had only functioned within the town.

There were also changes in the method of appointment, and in the type of men who held the office. Henry III's charter of 1267 merely said that the Prior and monks and their men should have coroners within the town, leaving the method of appointment open[4] but it seems virtually certain that the Prior appointed them: first because it was the usual custom for lords of liberties to do so,[5] and also that Roger de Pacwode's long period of office suggests the tenure of an appointment rather than a long series of favourable elections. Edward III's charter to the corporation, however, specifies that they should elect a coroner from amongst themselves *(de se ipsis).*[6] Throughout the fourteenth century the mercantile oligarchy who controlled the corporation did exactly that, regularly electing one of their own kind. There are no more clerks or lawyers: for the first forty years all the coroners whose occupations can be found are merchants. The last of these, Thomas de Nassyngton (coroner 1375-84) is also styled 'deyster', indicating one of those merchants organising the production of cloth who did their own dyeing. The rising status of the controllers of the cloth trade is further indicated by the election of a draper in 1387. A hosier succeeded him: William de Attleborough,[7] no humble fabricator of stockings but a man of sufficient wealth and status to become mayor later,[8] the first ex-coroner to do so. Three of the first four corporation coroners had been takers of building plots in Cheylesmore Park from Queen Isabella in 1348.[9] Most can be identified as members of the leading guilds and two, at least, were masters, Thomas de Nassyngton of St Mary's[10] and William de Attleborough of the great united Trinity Guild.[11]

The corporation was only fifteen months old when it secured the right to have a coroner, so the early holders of the office had not had the opportunity to be elected bailiff. Lesser corporation offices at that date are mostly unrecorded, and it is only through the survival of a single deed that we know that John de Baldeswell, the fourth coroner, had been chamberlain,[12] but six of the twelve coroners who followed did a term as bailiff, and, as we have seen, one of those, Attleborough, became mayor.[13] The draper Wyot never became bailiff, but for about two years was active as a presenting juror at Quarter Sessions.[14]

Clearly the corporation's coroners were prominent members of the ruling oligarchy, and it may be that the status of the men elected rose as we progress from the chamberlain John de Baldeswell to Attleburgh, a future mayor. One would very much like to have evidence about the effect, if any, of this close relationship with the city establishment on the coroners' performance of their duties, but we have only the negative evidence that so far no instances of extortion, corruption or inefficiency by the Coventry coroners have come to light. Examples elsewhere are plentiful, the commonest being refusals to hold inquests until a bribe, usually half a mark, had been paid. In the meantime the corpse lay unburied, in one case, for nine weeks. Eventually the bribe became an established and invariable fee.[15] As the coroner was officially unpaid, the temptation to extort illicit rewards was strong. However, if we are to believe the coroners' rolls, inquests in Coventry were held within two days of the finding of the body and sometimes on the same day.[16] Probably the Coventry coroners knew that their half mark would be forthcoming, and there are other factors making for efficiency: the social pressures on a coroner who was a well-known resident in a closely packed community would hardly have tolerated an unburied body, and the small area of the Coventry coroners' jurisdiction, which entailed, at the worst, a journey of five miles to Ansty, and in most cases only a fraction of that, made their task easier than that of their county colleagues.

Coroners frequently under-valued the forfeited chattels of felons, retaining the balance for themselves, and so robbing the royal Exchequer.[17] We have expressed our suspicions of the valuations in Coventry where it would be the corporation which was being robbed,[18] but whether to line the coroners' pockets or to protect the felons' dependents it is impossible to say. One further question must be asked: the coroner's office was unpaid, could be onerous, and carried the risk of amercement for failure in or neglect of duty. Why should Thomas de Nassyngton, having once been disqualified, accept office again and hold it for nine years? For prestige or the sense of power only?

The 'Incorporation Charter' of Edward III, 20 January 1345.
The charter of 1345 was a landmark in Coventry's history because it
greatly extended the rights of the townsmen. The men of Coventry were
to elect annually a mayor and bailiffs who were to have the hearing and
determination of all lawsuits and the custody of a prison for the
correction of wrongdoers. This is regarded as the first example of
municipal incorporation in Britain. The charter was granted at the
request of the King's mother, Queen Isabella, and out of consideration
for his son, Edward, Prince of Wales (later styled 'The Black Prince') to
whom the manor of Coventry was to pass at his grandmother's death.
The first mayor, John Ward, is mentioned in a deed of 1346 since when
there has been a continuous line of mayors and, from 1953, lord mayors
in the City. BA/G/A/3/1. *Reproduced courtesy of Coventry Archives.*

Table 2: The Corporation's Coroners: reigns of Edward III and Richard II

First reference as coroner		Last reference as coroner
John de Arthingworth, merchant[19]	18 Jan 1347[20]	24 Dec 1347[21]
John le Waller, wool merchant[22]	8 May 1349[23]	11 May 1349[24]
John Box	6 Feb 1350[25]	29 Apr 1354[26]
John de Baldeswell, merchant[27]	25 Jan 1355[28]	20 Oct 1358[29]
Ralph Huitt	26 Apr 1362[30]	
Robert de Bruggeford	5 Oct 1362[31]	24 Jun 1364[32]
Wm Palmer (see JUST $^3/_4$ S2m19 - one of coroners for Warks.		
Thos de Baldeswell	Before 19 Feb 1369[33]	c. 3 Mar 1369[34]
Thomas de Nassington, merchant, dyer[35]		Removed 3 Mar 1370[36]

Wm de Ocham, merchant[37]	Before 19 Jul 1370[38]	20 Mar 1373
Thos de Nassington	Before 22 Feb 1375[39]	c. 28 Feb 1384[40]
Thomas de Sutton	6 Feb 1386[41]	
John Wyot, draper	19 Sep 1387[43]	25 Jan 1390[44]
Roger de Wedon, ?brewer/innkeeper[45]	21 May 1390[46]	c. 2 Jun 1390[47]
Wm de Attelburgh, hosier[48]	25 Jan 1391[49]	25 Jan 1394[50] (sic)
John Houlond	29 Sep 1393[51] (sic)	25 Jan 1397[52]
Philip Baron, merchant[53]	4 Apr 1397[54]	

Note: The coroner did not regularly witness deeds in the mayor's court as he had done in the Prior's, so there is no continuous record from which the names of the coroners after 1346 can be discovered until the Leet Book records their election from 1421 onwards.

Appendix

John de Arthingworth

The first corporation coroner, John de Arthingworth, was the last of his line to be prominent in Coventry. The family was established in the city by about 1268,[55] but no sons survived John when he died during the Black Death, and the surname does not appear afterwards. The Arthingworth's base was Gosford Street, where John and his two unmarried sisters had separate properties.[56] In Far Gosford Street, John had two messuages on the north side with a cottage between them.[57] He also had a tenement between Gosford bridges which he leased to tenants until 1335, when he conveyed it to Alice, widow of John de Langleye and her second husband Henry Geddyng.[58] The following year he conveyed another Gosford Street property to Agnes Uttyng and her son Richard, charging it with a rent secured to himself.[59] On the slope between his Far Gosford Street properties and Harnall lay Ludlowe's Field, where, on Christmas Eve 1345, Arthingworth took over Robert de Lodelowe's holding on an interesting lease: Arthingworth was to farm the land and harvest the corn, and after tithe had been taken, deliver a third of the remaining sheaves to Lodelowe's house in Coventry. This arrangement was to run for twelve years; after that Arthingworth could, if he wished, retain the land for life at a rent of £10 a year (later reduced to £5).[60] He had other unspecified land in Coventry on lease[61] and his holdings extended beyond the city limits into the adjoining manor of Stoke, where he witnessed deeds, including an important one where the current lord, John de Stoke, assigned the manor to his mother as her dower.[62] Slightly further afield Arthingworth had property in Whitley and Binley.[63] He had some sort of footing in the city centre as his tenement is mentioned as a boundary in Greyfriars Lane.[64] In 1338 he was one of eight men being sued in the Court of Common Pleas by John atte Clyf, possibly in connection with a holding in Gosford Street for which he was paying three shillings rent to Philip atte Clif in 1341.[65]

Two earlier Arthingworths were drapers[66] but we do not know what trade John engaged in, only that he was styled merchant when he took one of the plots in Cheylesmore Park from Queen Isabella.[67] He was a frequent witness to deeds, but until he became coroner, they all related to the Gosford-Stoke-Lodelowe's Field area,[68] giving the impression of a local worthy in that area rather than a man involved with the property acquisitions of the great guilds throughout the city, and while he and his wife were guild members, he is unlikely to have been one of the controlling elite. This and his modest contributions to the subsidies (two shillings in 1327, one shilling and fourpence in 1332)[69] suggest a man of middling wealth and status able to spare the time for the duties of his (officially) unpaid office. His election as the corportion's first coroner may have owed something to a link with the wool merchant John de Ruisshale whom he appointed one of his trustees to dispose of his property after his death. Ruisshale was one of 'the Twelve' who, through Isabella, purchased the corporation's right to their own coroner.[70]

Arthingworth first appears as a witness in 1321,[71] so he must have been in early middle age when he took office. He appears twice in the list of guild members, first with his wife Joan, and again with 'his wife' unnamed. This, together with the disposition of some of his estate after his death suggests that he was a member of both St Mary's and St John the Baptist's guilds.[72] He must have married twice, as his widow was Lucy when he died in 1349[73], probably of the Black Death. His last recorded act, on March 8th, was to convey his property to Ruisshale and Henry Pane (who had been bailiffs together in 1348), except for the cottage in Far Gosford Street obviously intended to be a home for Lucy and Joan, John's daughter. Joan, as heiress, inherited the cottage, but on April 14th she gave it (together with a rent of two shillings a year from another house) to Lucy, who was probably her stepmother. The Black Death was by this time rising to its peak in Coventry, and the fact that Joan found it necessary to delegate Pane to perform the formal handing over probably indicates that she was already sick. On May 10th Lucy conveyed the cottage to the Master, chaplain, and another member of St Mary's guild, and on the 26th she relinquished the lease of the land in Ludlowe's Field.[74] 'The rest is silence': we have found no later reference to any living members of the Arthingworth family.

Though Arthingworth's trustees acted quickly, it is unlikely that they completed the disposal of his estate before they too succumbed to the pestilence. Five days after Arthingworth's conveyance to them, Ruisshale and Pane conveyed a rent of four shillings a year from three cottages between Gosford bridges to the Master and four brethren of St Mary's guild.[75] A similar rent was due to Arthingworth from three cottages in the same area owned by St John the Baptist's guild, and this was conveyed to three chaplains who were guild members.[76] Pane probably died in late April or early May as there is no record of him after April 27th and on May 11th Ruisshale acted alone to convey one of the houses in Gosford Street to Richard and Pernelle de Welford.[77] In June he gave a rent of twenty shillings, charged on some of the Arthingworth properties, to three chaplains, two of whom were members of St Mary's guild,[78] for which the rent was no doubt intended. A considerable amount of property still remained in Ruisshale's hands, but as there are no further references to him it is likely that he also fell victim to the plague.

John le Waller

During the Black Death the Coventrians did not panic to the pitch of abandoning the attempt to keep the city's administration going: Arthingworth died before April 14th and by May 8th the wool merchant John le Waller had been elected coroner.[79] He was the son of William le Waller[80] who, with his brother Geoffrey, was the first of the family to be recorded in Coventry. Their base was Spon Street, where the brothers first appear in the last decade of the thirteenth century and where John had three messuages, a tenement and some rents,[81] but they also had a footing in the city centre, for Geoffrey and William were among those prosecuted by the Prior in 1307 for selling cloth in Earl Street on market days.[82] They may only have had a booth or stall there, but John had a messuage in Broadgate in 1349.[83]

The market case was the only occasion when Geoffrey was in conflict with the Prior, but William was in the thick of the opposition in 1323, and the next year was one of those accused of besieging the Priory and seeking to encompass the Prior's death by witchcraft. With him in this was John the future coroner, said in 1324 to be serving Alice le Hunte,[84] a wealthy widow and a wool merchant on her own account. No doubt the experience gained as her employee was put to use when John entered the wool trade himself. By 1332 he was one of the seven Coventry merchants living at Bruges in Flanders along with 35 others from various parts of England who were in trouble with the English government for trying to make Bruges the staple town through which all English wool must be exported. At that particular juncture Edward III's administration favoured free trade in wool, and the merchants in Bruges were ordered to release the wool of a Bridgnorth merchant which they had impounded, and allow him to sell it where he pleased. As they proved recalcitrant the sheriffs of London were ordered to seize any wool or goods they could find belonging to the Coventrians and others.[85] Waller was now an active member of the mercantile community: in 1335 he acknowleged in Chancery a debt of £40 owed to John de Weston, another Coventry merchant who had been in Bruges;[86] two years later he was being sued in the Common Pleas by the Earl Street merchant Richard atte Grene to account for money handled as Grene's agent or employee. Grene alleged that Waller had been entrusted with a certain sum to trade on Grene's behalf, the cash being handed over partly in Coventry and partly in London, and that Waller had not accounted. Waller denied liability and a trial was ordered for a later date before a mixed jury of Londoners and men from Warwickshire, but the case dragged on into the next year.[87] Cases of account and debt between Coventry merchants were common enough and Waller was not the only man to be sued by Grene.[88] Three years later St Mary's merchant guild was founded and its first Master, Jordan de Shepeye (who had also been at Bruges in 1332[89]), began with Henry Dodenhale to acquire property on the guild's behalf. Waller's witnessing of a deed whereby Shepeye and Dodenhale granted a rent from a holding on the site of the future St Mary's Hall, and his appearance with his wife near the head of the list of Johns in the Trinity Guild Register bespeak his early involvement with the guild.[90] Not surprisingly, he was one of the merchants who took plots in Cheylesmore Park in 1348.[91]

Waller's career as a coroner was dramatically brief: he first witnessed as coroner on May 8th 1349, and for the last time three days later.[92] Even if he was elected immediately after Arthingworth's death in March or April, he can only have been coroner for a few weeks, when, in his last recorded act, on May

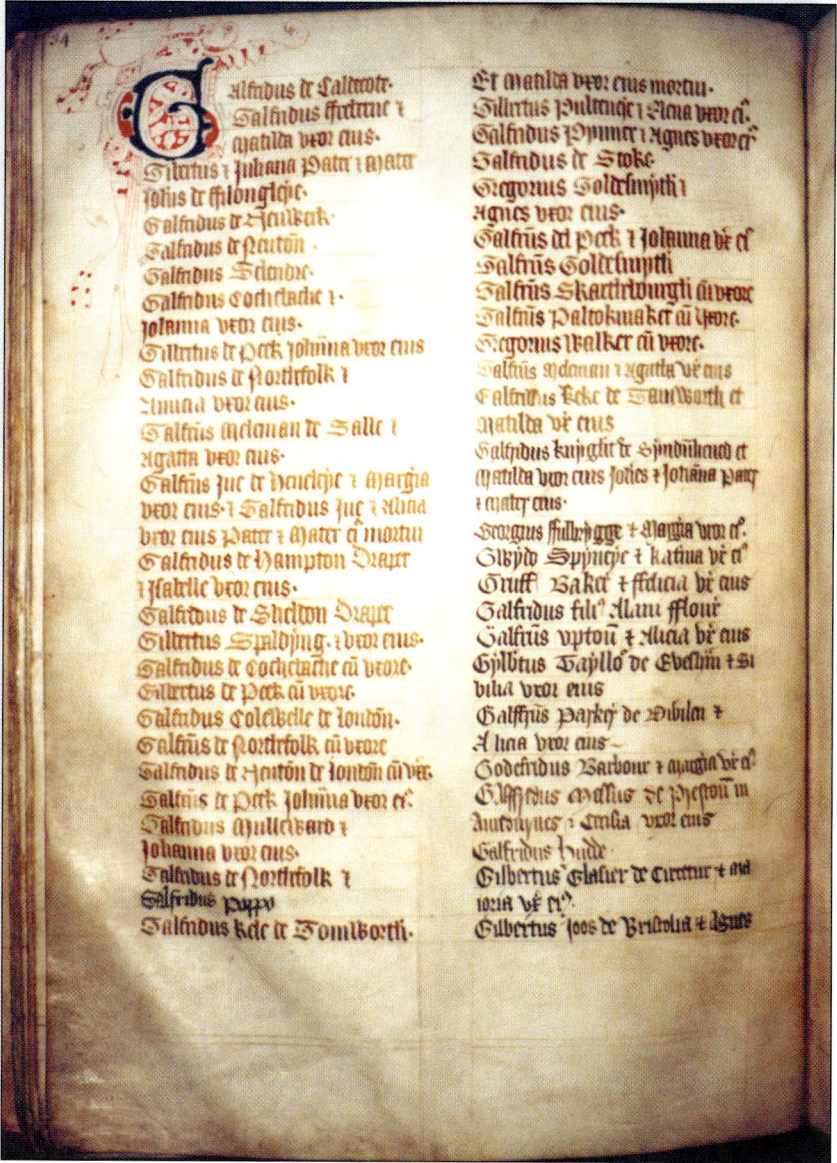

The Trinity Guild Register, 1400-1450.
Formed in 1364 the Trinity Guild absorbed those of St Mary's, St John the Baptist and St Katherine, their union being officially confirmed in 1392. It is a nominal register (retrospective from c.1350) arranged alphachronologically according to Christian name, it features the urban middle class, male and female, together with national dignitaries and merchants outside Coventry. Mary Dormer Harris, the Coventry historian edited the Trinity Guild Register as Vol.XIII of Dugdale Society main series, produced in 1935. PA18. *Reproduced courtesy of Coventry Archives.*

16th, he gave his property to two trustees, Henry Ballard and a chaplain, John de Southam. Ballard does not appear again and presumably was a plague victim as we find Southam alone disposing of the property. In August he conveyed two of the Spon Street messuages to the next Master, two chaplains, and another member of St Mary's guild,[93] followed in 1352 by a rent of four shillings and eightpence from a tenement in the same street, conveyed to the Master and a chaplain.[94] Meanwhile another Spon Street rent had been conveyed to the corporation's chamberlains, John de Baldeswell, the future coroner, and Henry Dilcok.[95] The similarity between the disposals of the two coroners' estates will be obvious. There is nothing, however, to link Waller with St John the Baptist's guild.

John Box

In Arthingworth and Waller we have depicted the type of men who became the corporation's coroners. It would be tedious to continue with full details of all their successors in the fourteenth century, but some items of significance or interest will enhance our description. Waller's successor, John Box, attracts attention by his contribution of a mark (thirteen shillings and fourpence) to the Lay Subsidy of 1332, which puts him in a different category from the other early coroners who paid, and places him among the wealthiest quarter of Coventry subsidy payers: of 135 taxed, fourteen paid a mark, and only fifteen paid more.[96] When the levy was taken for Edward II's campaign against Lancaster in 1322, Box seems to have been a partner in some sort of enterprise, as a contribution was recorded from 'John Box and his fellows *(sociis suis)*.'[97] Unfortunately the amount they paid cannot now be read. Box's links with the new corporation are evidenced by his appearance as defendant in the important 'cognisance of pleas' case in 1346. Ostensibly this was an action brought in the Court of Common Pleas by Henry Ballard to gain possession of a messuage held by Box, his brother- in-law. But the action was collusive, a test case to establish the corporation's right under their new charter to try such cases in the mayor and bailiffs' court.[98]

Thomas de Nassyngton

With Box's successor, John de Baldeswell, who paid two shillings in 1327[99] we come to the end of the coroners whose relative wealth can be surmised from their contributions to the lay subsidies, and we have to use other clues, sometimes tenuous, to their economic and social status. Next in time come the prosecutions by two future coroners under the Statute of Labourers in 1355, which show Robert de Bruggeford (coroner 1362-64) to have had a maid-servant *(ancilla)* (who was fined), while Thomas de Nassyngton prosecuted two weavers who presumably had done work for him.[100] These links with the weavers suggest that he was the dyer who appears with his wife Juliana in the Trinity Guild Register, but his more usual style of 'merchant' indicates one of those dyers who organised the manufacture and sale of cloth rather than a man with his own hands in the dye vat.[101] Nassyngton's is the only case we know of where the Coventrians' choice of coroner was over-ruled by the central administration. Most likely he was elected on January 25th 1370, but in March a writ was issued from Chancery removing him as insufficiently qualified.[102] Most commonly this would mean that he was not wealthy enough: coroners were officially unpaid and so needed land or other possessions to live on, and also must have the resources to be able to pay fines to the king or damages to injured parties if they failed or were corrupt in their duties. Burgesses who elected impoverished coroners were liable to be mulcted for the fines and damages themselves.[103] Nassyngton had already been master of the leading guild, St Mary's, and also bailiff,[104] both offices normally held by men of substance. He could have suffered a financial disaster or had opponents in Coventry who alleged his insufficiency. Certainly he is unlikely to have been one of those elected coroners against his will, who got themselves disqualified to escape service, for when he was elected again five years later, he served for at least nine years, longer than any other corporation coroner before 1400, so presumably he liked the job.[105]

Nassyngton's involvement with the affairs of St Mary's guild, and, after the merger, with the Trinity guild, was probably typical of the men whom the Coventrians elected coroners in the second half of the fourteenth century, though not all are as well documented. Besides his mastership of St Mary's, he figures as one of those in whom the legal ownership of guild property was vested, either as trustees or to facilitate conveyances or leases.[106] In 1376 he obtained a valuable lease of guild property himself: a lease for life or forty years, whichever was longer, of a messuage, barn, sixteen selions of arable and half a grove. Some of the selions lay near the lane from the White Friars to the Altogether Mill. An amended lease a year later omitted the barn but added another nineteen selions. The rent was fifty shillings a year for the first forty years, a hundred shillings thereafter.[107] Ten of the sixteen fourteenth-century corporation coroners appear in the Trinity Guild Register. The absence of the other six[108] from the Register does not, however, prove that they were not members, for the list is not perfect, and some undoubted guild members are missing.[109] William de Ocham, coroner from 1370 to 1373, does not appear there, but he was involved in several guild transactions and was one of the feoffees of the Drapery on the guild's behalf.[110]

William de Attleburgh

For the last decade of the century the Coventry Statute Merchant Roll on which the recognisances of debts were recorded, gives us glimpses of the financial status and problems of two coroners: in February 1397, a Coventry shoemaker owed Philip Baron £200, to be paid at Michaelmas that year. As nothing more is recorded we can perhaps assume that Baron got his money. William de Attleburgh was not so fortunate. A carpenter and his son, both called John de Haddon, owed him £24 in September 1393, to be paid on Christmas Eve. Alas, by April 1395 they were owing £44 *(sic)*. But they are eclipsed as defaulting debtors by Attleburgh's fellow hosier John Blykeleye of Worcestershire. On August 7th 1395 he owed Attleburgh £14 10s to be paid a week later: fifteen years on it was still owing,[111] and Attleburgh obtained a certificate of non-payment, the first step in a process leading to the transfer of a debtor's lands to his creditor.[112] In the interval Attleburgh had been Master of the Trinity Guild and Mayor,[113] but two years of public office can hardly have been the reason for his not taking action sooner.

Chapter 4: The Jurors

Finally, the jurors, called together for the grisly chore of viewing the body before giving the verdict which could put a man on trial for his life. The first thing that strikes us is how numerous they were. Between February 1355 and October 1358 the coroner, John de Baldeswell, conducted thirty inquests within the town and two outside, in Keresley and Foleshill, and 249 men were called on for the town inquests.[1] There is a gap in the records until October 1362 when Robert de Bruggesford's roll begins and covers two years. Thirty of the jurors who served under Baldeswell appear again but there are 179 new names,[2] making 429 for about six years. Some must have served between 1358 and 1362, but it is reasonable to estimate eighty extra names for each of the missing years, that is, about 750 jurors over a decade, more than a third of the men living in Coventry.[3] During an adult life of, say, twenty-five years a man must have had a better than even chance of serving on a coroner's inquest, and this was the most likely way a Coventrian of lowly status might participate in the processes of the law. He was much more likely to be chosen for a coroner's inquest than to be either one of the presenting jurors or of the group of constables who also presented offenders before the justices of the peace at their quarterly sessions. For the last quarter of the fourteenth century we have both coroners' and quarter sessions rolls, albeit in broken series:144 men, served on the inquests taken in the town during John Wyot's term as coroner in 1388-90.[4] Under a fifth of them presented as jurors or constables at quarter sessions in the seven years between 1377 and 1397 for which we have records.[5]

The number of coroner's jurors was large partly because of the frequency of inquests, but more because it was not the practice to call repeatedly on the same man. Because of the gaps in the rolls we cannot say with certainty how often individuals served, but it is clear that the great majority only acted once: of the 249 town jurors on Baldeswell's roll, only 76 are recorded as having served twice or more under under either Baldeswell or Bruggeford. Eighteen of these acted three times and only two (or possibly three) four times.[6] We have seen that jurors were chosen because they were likely to know something about the death. There was no reason for them to serve again unless they had knowledge of another, which seems to have been the case with Alexander Styward: in 1358 he was a juror at the inquest of a woman accidentally drowned in the Sherbourne. His only other appearance is five years later when a girl had fallen from the river bank. Perhaps he lived near the Sherbourne. John Swon, whose only jury service was when John de Thedyworth died of natural causes in a field by St Nicholas church, had land opposite the church.[7] Not only were the numbers large, but almost all levels of society were involved, because of the very numbers and because of selection on account of accidental knowledge of such deaths. From deeds and other documents relating to the thirty years before 1357, the names of over three thousand Coventrians have been gleaned, mostly owners, lessees and trustees of houses or land or witnesses to conveyances. But half the jurors on Baldeswell's roll are not among them. Of course in six hundred years many documents have been lost, but it seems likely that many of our jurors were not owners or lessees of real property. The occupations of a mere thirteen of the 249 jurors are given on Baldeswell's roll. The trades of thirty others are given in the contemporary records of the justices of labourers,[8] the list of those granted land in Cheylesmore Park in 1348,[9] and in deeds[10] and other documents. There were three tailors and the same number of weavers, two each of shoemakers, hosiers, mercers, butchers and slaters. There was a single wiredrawer, smith, cartwright, mason, tiler, thatcher, skinner, hatter, whittawer, glover, girdler, woolmonger, sherman, dyer and draper, an inn-keeper, and Adam, servant of the Master of St John's Hospital.[11] William de Kyngeston in Greyfriars Lane, had presumably retired from his craft or business as he was enjoying a corrody, perhaps from the Greyfriars.

While the styles given to these men indicate the trades with which they were involved, it is only when other information is available that we can know their position in them and deduce their wealth or poverty. The 'woolmonger', John de Pakinton[13] presumably needed considerable working capital, and one would expect the innkeeper, William Cook at the Whitecellar, one of the largest inns in the town, to be a man of substance, even though he was a tenant and not the owner.[14] The trades of draper and mercer were not for poor men: one mercer, William de Cayvile, a future mayor,[15] the other, John Chaloner, was assumed to be able to pay a 4 shilling fine for poaching.[16] But with other occupations the one-word style gives no clue as to whether the juror was a wage-earner, a craftsman working on his own account or an employer who might in another context be called a merchant, like the skinner, Sewall de Bulkington, a future bailiff, who had been Master of St Mary's Guild, and in 1347 was summoned with other merchants to attend the king's council for consultations about the wool trade.[17] The hosier, Richard Frebern, was probably the merchant who was bailiff in the year of the Black Death, and mayor the next year,[18] and there were seven or eight other merchants so styled.[19]

The records of the justices of labourers help us to identify some jurors as artisans who were presented or fined for taking excess pay (or for refusing to take the oath which inhibited them from so doing) or as those who employed them or complained about them.[20] Artisans' fines, when levied, were 6d or 12d. The tiler, John de Kent, a juror, was fined 12d, and his 'servant' (i.e. mate or labourer) 6d. Besides Kent another dozen jurors belong to this group. William de Lutterworth, his servant Richard de Fillongley, both fined 20d, and John de Colleshull (40d) were higher up the economic ladder, and Thomas de la More who failed to appear before the justices had property to be distrained on, for the justices extracted 12d from the issues.[21] Eleven jurors were on the other side of the economic divide, as employers, prosecutors or complainants against those who tried to improve their pay. We know no more about some of them than we do of the artisans. Nicholas Gopil, for instance, whose servant Alice demanded thirty shillings a year, was twice a juror[22] but we know nothing more of him, and three others are equally obscure, but the eleven include Thomas de Nassyngton, a future coroner and bailiff,[23] John de Norhampton, a prosperous butcher,[24] and Henry Mollyng, a founder of the Holy Cross Chantry and currently or very recently Master of St John the Baptist's guild.[25] We are now among the property owners and establishment figures, and our information goes beyond the records of the justices of labourers: deeds and other documents identify over 40 of Baldeswell's 249 jurors as owners or lessees of houses and land,[26] and no doubt further research would add to the list. Among them were nine of the elite.

Besides Nassyngton, there was Richard Freburn, already mentioned, and Henry de Kele, a founder and Master of Holy Trinity Guild, bailiff, four times mayor and a leading J.P.[27] Only Frebum had most of his career behind him. Kele was a rising young man who became bailiff fourteen and mayor twenty-five years later. The other seven, Nassyngton, Sewall de Bulkinton, William Cayvile, Adam de Keresleye, Edward Wedon, Thomas le Parker and Gilbert del Peek became bailiffs after shorter intervals,[28] but may have already filled minor corporation offices, while Bulkinton and Nassyngton had been Masters of St Mary's Guild.[29] Their eminence did not entail extra calls for jury service. Cayvile served three times, but the other eight made only eleven appearances between them. It is interesting, however, that most of their service was concentrated in a few inquests where three or four of them served together. When the mercer, Thomas Shakespeare, killed the Warwick goldsmith Robert de Kyngton in Coventry, Cayvile, Freburn, Nassyngton and Parker were on the jury, plus William de Wendleburgh, who was one of 'the Twelve'; when another mercer, William Prest, was killed by John de Norhampton, the jury which returned a verdict of self-defence included Peek, Kele and Bulkinton, while Kele, Keresleye and Wedon were called on when the ironmonger William de Sutton had been robbed and fatally wounded at Gupill's ford.[30] Perhaps the notabilities were selected as being the social and economic equals of the victims or assailants, and so presumed to have useful knowledge. The suspicion of jury-rigging inevitably arises, but unfortunately we have no evidence to corroborate or contradict this.

Wendleburgh was the most eminent member of a jury assembled on October 15th 1355 to investigate the death of a man found dead 'in a certain place called Bisshepeshall' a fortnight after being hit with a staff. Wendleburgh and three other jurors, Henry Whitmore, John Baxter and Richard de Fillongleye,[31] were involved in the Fraternity of the Holy Cross and its chantry in Holy Trinity Church. The fraternity held its annual feast in a building between Bishop Street and Cook Street in the Prior's Half.[32] Although the Bishop's Hall (aula episcopi) did exist at the northeast corner of St Michael's churchyard,[33] the date of the inquest late in the year of the Tripartite Indenture, which provided for the corporation's coroner to function in the Prior's Half,[34] and the presence of the

A trial showing prosecution witness giving evidence, early 15th Century.
North France, early 15th century. MS. Rawl. Liturg.e.12, F.142v.
Book of Vlairs.
Reproduced courtesy of the Bodleian Library, University of Oxford.

51

Holy Cross members on the jury lead one to think that this was the first inquest under the new agreement and that the death took place in the Bishop's Half, as the Prior's part was still sometimes called in English in the fourteenth century,[35] and that the scribe who compiled the coroner's roll from the original files over thirty years later wrote 'Bisshepeshall' in error.[36]

Obviously occasional service on a coroner's inquest was not burdensome, especially when the duty was spread among all ranks of Coventry citizens. Apparently neither wealth nor poverty excused men or increased their liability to serve. While exact statistical comparisons are not possible, it likely that the 'pyramid' of jurors, with its broad base of obscure people and a peak formed by a few civic notables, reflects approximately the composition of the city's population.

Part 2: The Justices of the Peace

Chapter 5: The Powers and Personnel of the Commission of the Peace

Late medieval kings and parliaments struggled, without conspicuous success, with the problems of violence and disorder 'Forasmuch as from day to day robberies, murders, arson are more often committed than they used to be' began the Statute of Winchester of 1285, which made the local community pay compensation to the victims of robberies on its territory. It was hoped that the fear of being fined would encourage jurors at views of frankpledge and other courts to denounce the malefactors, sheriffs, bailiffs and constables to arrest them, and the men of the community, suitably armed, to pursue when the hue and cry was raised.[1] This was an attempt to give a new impetus to the ancient machinery of justice and law enforcement, but it soon became clear that the old institutions were not enough by themselves to overcome the current surge of crime and disorder, and in the first half of the fourteenth century several experiments were tried: appointing commissioners of 'trailbaston', charged with the discovery and arrest of vagrant cudgel-bearing gangs who lurked in the countryside and attacked people at markets and fairs,[2] and commissioners to enquire about specific felonies and trespasses or about all such felonies and trespasses in a particular area.[3]

With hindsight we know that the most promising development was the appointment of local knights and gentlemen as keepers of the peace. Though these had appeared spasmodically before 1285, it had not been envisaged that they would be used to enforce the Statute of Winchester. But during the reign of Edward II appointments became more frequent, and by 1327 enforcement of the King's Peace and the Statute had become a regular clause in their commissions. They were to enquire, by sworn inquest about the felonies and trespasses, and arrest those responsible. They were not, however, empowered to try them, but handed them over to the sheriff to await trial in prison.[4]

The Coventry keepers make a brief appearance in the records of June 1357, when they turned out (accompanied by William atte Hoo with a lighted candle), to attempt the arrest of a burglar after the hue and cry had been raised.[5] But by this time the conversion of the keepers into justices of the peace was well on the way, though not consolidated by statute until 1360.[6] King, Council and Parliament wrangled over their powers, but by 1368 they included trial and punishment of felonies and trespasses, supervision of weights and measures, and the powers formerly exercised by the Justices of Labourers.[7] Trying felonies meant the power to have men hanged, so it was customary to augment the local justices by including in the commission eminent professional lawyers, usually judges, one of whom must be present when felonies were tried. In the earliest period for which we have records of the Coventry J.P.s sessions, the two decades after 1377, most of the eminent lawyers did not sit, except for Thomas Purfrey, who was a local man, and recorder of Coventry,[8] and up to 1399 it is unlikely that the town's justices ever hanged anyone. They took the indictments of alleged felons and committed them to prison to await trial by the itinerant royal judges. Those judges who were named in the commission probably preferred to deal with felonies in their own courts of gaol delivery rather than with amateurs in quarter session. In 1399 a new charter for Coventry provided that in future the justices of the peace should be the mayor, recorder, and four men chosen by the mayor, but they were forbidden to try felonies except by the king's special writ.[9]

Normally then, the J.P.s, meeting four times a year, tried cases of 'trespass'. These were not however the simple cases involving remedies or damages for aggrieved plaintiffs, as in the Cheylesmore court baron. A breach of the king's peace, or of a statute, must be alleged, making the offence an indictable trespass, as it was called before the lawyers invented the term 'misdemeanour'. But reluctance to make serious offences hanging matters by including 'the words of felony' in the indictment meant that they were classed as trespasses: assaults, housebreaking, taking and detaining goods (stopping short of larceny, which was a felony), resisting arrest, helping prisoners to escape, threats and extortions, all came under the same judicial umbrella of trespass.[10]

The justices punished the trespassers, by fine or imprisonment, but they had no power to award damages.[11] Obviously some aggrieved parties would have to choose between the satisfaction of seeing their adversaries punished by the J.P.s or getting compensation in another court. Offences against the Statute of Labourers was a special case. When these were finally turned over to the J.P.s in 1368, they were empowered to award the damages 'according to the quantity of the trespass', presumably meaning the refund of excess wages or prices ordered by the Statute.[12]

The first commission of the peace for Coventry was issued on February 28th 1354, and sixteen others followed by the end of the century.[13] Amongst the towns, only Beverley had more, eighteen beginning in 1352. Next comes York with fourteen. Perhaps these small variations are not significant - probably commissions were issued as needed. If the King and Council were satisfied with the justices and there were no complaints about them, there was no need to change them. What is more interesting is that these towns seem to have had J.P.s in office for most of the second half of the century, while, for instance, at Leicester there is a single commission in November 1356, and at Lincoln, only two, in 1351 and 1380. Other towns were similarly spasmodic.[14] Presumably, in their case, the mayors or bailiffs in their ancient local courts upheld the king's peace, or the county J.P.s covered the town, as they did for Coventry for six years following the suspension of all urban commissions of the peace after the Peasants' Revolt of 1381.[15]

Who were the J.P.s who wielded such power over delinquent Coventrians? Over fifty years ago, Dr Elisabeth Kimball pointed out that the justices commissioned for Coventry in the last quarter of the century belonged to four groups: peers, gentry, burgesses of Coventry, and lawyers, though no single commission included all four groups.[16] Surveying all known commissions from 1354 to the end of the century, we can ignore the two peers who feature in the last five years: the inclusion of Thomas de Beauchamp, earl of Warwick, and his replacement in 1397 by John Holand, duke of Exeter, merely reflect the shifts in the relationships between Richard II and his magnates. The earl took no part in the J.P.s' proceedings, and it is unlikely that the duke did, but the records of his commission have not survived.[17] The first Coventry commission, of 1354,[18] names seven men, beginning with two eminent lawyers, Green and Skipwith, judges of the Court of Common Pleas, accustomed to travelling the country as justices of assize or gaol delivery.[19] As we have said, it is unlikely that they ever sat as J.P.s. Four eminent Coventrians follow: Walter Whitewebbe, the mayor, Nicholas Michel, who had been mayor at the time of the Black Death, and was to hold the office another three times, Richard Frebern, who had followed Michel as mayor in 1350,[20] and John de Meryngton. The last was a member of the family of wool merchants who had estates in rural Warwickshire as well as property in Coventry,[21] and he seems to have taken little interest in city affairs. He was never mayor or bailiff, and, while his mother was a member of one of the guilds, probably St Mary's,[22] it seems that he was not. Most of Meryngton's public appointments were in Warwickshire where he was on the commission of the peace in 1345 and a commissioner to levy the subsidy,[23] but he was one of the commissioners to enquire into the Coventry riot against the assessment for the King's loan in 1351.[24] In his youth he was one of those accused in the witchcraft case of 1323, when he was described as an apprentice of the king's court,[25] but there is no evidence of his being a practising lawyer.

The remaining justice was Hugh de Aston, apparently not a Coventrian, but a justice of the peace or of labourers in six Midland counties, and for Shrewsbury as well as Coventry.[26] Like Meryngton he had been a commissioner to enquire into the Coventry riot already mentioned,[27] and was on other commissions to hear and determine alleged crimes.[28] Two ecclesiastics, the bishop of London in 1354, and the Prior of St Mary's, Worcester the next year, nominated him as their attorney in England whilst they were abroad.[29] Probably he was a professional lawyer, and certainly he was regarded as the leading J.P., as the account of the fines which the justices sent to the Exchequer was headed 'Fines before Hugh de Aston and his fellows'[30] - another indication that the judges Green and Skipwith did not sit. From 1368 onwards, one justice, perhaps the leading one, was designated *custos rotulorum* (keeper of the rolls).[31] For the rest of the reign of Edward III, the leading justice was someone whose public life was not centred on Coventry,[32] though he might have property there, as William de Catesby who followed Aston certainly did.[33] In the first commission of Richard ll's reign, however, John Percy, a former mayor, was made custos, followed in 1380 by Adam Botoner,[34] twice mayor and traditionally one of the builders of St Michael's tower. A handful of gentry having no obvious connections with Coventry were included in the city's commissions of the peace, especially in the 1370s, but they were not numerous enough to dominate the bench even if they had been diligent in attendance.

From 1354 to 1370 it was customary, when a new commission was issued, to include the current mayor, but he was not included on the four commissions issued between 1374 and 1377. Whatever the reason, the omissions made little difference in practice to the composition of the bench. The mayors were not superseded as justices by the new mayor at the end of their mayoralty, which might have only a few months to run when the commission was issued. So, even when we include the mayoralties of Nicholas Michel (in 1356) and Henry Clerk (1363), who were already J.P.s when they took office, the current mayor was on the commission for only about a quarter of the time between February 1354 and November 1374. But there was almost always an ex-mayor among the justices. From 1380 the practice of including the current mayor was resumed,[35] until 1399 when Richard ll's charter provided that thenceforth the mayor, the recorder and four others chosen by the mayor were to be the J.P.s,[36] as has already been mentioned. The Coventrians could now exclude the Warwickshire gentry from the city's quarter sessions. The inclusion of prominent figures from the corporation in the commission of the peace must have helped to maintain a working relationship between two potentially conflicting jurisdictions. The mayor and bailiffs as well as the J.P.s had power to punish economic offences,[37] and both took indictments of felons who were sent for trial before the justices of gaol delivery. The bailiffs were responsible for the gaol to which both they and the J.P.s committed those indicted.[38] But if there was friction, there is no sign of it in the J.P.s' records, except for one instance where a bailiff tore up one of their indictments.[39]

The stipulation in 1399 that the recorder must be one of the justices formalised the established custom of having on the commission a lawyer with local connections, who would be more readily available than the royal judges; the Coventry commission of

February 1367 named only three J.P.s, William de Catesby, the mayor Richard de Stoke, and Nicholas Michel, already three times mayor, and like Catesby, an experienced J.P. Unusually, no judges were included but in the following November Richard de Sheldon was added to the commission.[40] Richard and Thomas de Sheldon were professional attorneys who represented Coventry clients, amongst others, in the Court of Common Pleas at Westminster,[41] and Richard was the mayor's and bailiffs' attorney before the justices of assize at Warwick in 1350.[42] The judges reappeared on the Coventry commission in 1368, but Richard Sheldon remained a J.P. until 1376.[43] No obvious successor can be discerned until the lawyer Thomas Purefrey was appointed in 1387. He was also a J.P. for Warwickshire and recorder of Coventry, where he sat regularly and remained on the commission of the peace until the end of the century.[44]

As we have seen, after the Peasants' Revolt, the Coventry commission was suspended,[45] and in 1384-85 the county J.P.s sat in the city to deal with local offenders.[46] By January 1384 however, the government had regained confidence in the Coventrians to the extent that they added three ex-mayors, Adam Botoner, John Percy, and John Tofts to the Warwickshire commission.[47] The intention must surely have been that they would take part when the county J.P.s sat in the city, but they do not appear to have done so.[48] Nonetheless it was becoming accepted that Coventry malefactors could be tried before their own leading citizens: from 1387, when the city got its own justices again, until Richard II's charter of 1399 only mayors or ex- mayors, plus Thomas Purefrey, actually sat although judges and peers were named in the commissions,[49] as we have seen. Until 1377 we have no means of knowing how many or which of the justices named in the commission actually sat. From then on, the maximum number at any session in the surviving records is four. More usually three or sometimes only two were present.[50] So a delinquent Coventrian would face a bench of one, two or three city fathers, often, but not always reinforced by a Warwickshire gentleman or lawyer.

How far, territorially, did the authority of the Coventry justices extend? The earlier commissions were simply for the town of Coventry, but from 1380 they covered the town and suburbs.[51] It would seem neat and logical if the whole area of the Cheylesmore view of frankpledge, over which the mayor and bailiffs had been given some jurisdiction in 1345, had coincided with the area overseen by the city's J.P.s. But at first that was not the case, for in 1381 we find the Warwickshire justices (who had received and obeyed the the instructions not to meddle with cases in the Coventry suburbs) , dealing with a case of cattle rustling at Caludon and an assault at Foleshill,[52] both within the jurisdiction of the Cheylesmore leet, but not, obviously, yet within the Coventry J.P.s' area. A smaller area wherein the mayor and bailiffs were to exercise the authority which they had within the city was defined by the Black Prince's charter of 1375.[53] It included, for instance, Whitley, Shortley and Coundon, but not Stoke or Wyken, from where, again in 1381, cases of theft and robbery came before the Coventry sessions. Stoke is correctly described in the presentment as 'by' *(iuxta)* Coventry, but a clerk wrote later in the margin 'Stoke within the town of Coventry' (which it was not, topographically), while the highway robbery was located 'at *(apud)* Coventry upon Wyken Green', which in the fourteenth century was ridiculous.[54] The point of these descriptions must surely have been that the two villages were part of the suburbs where the town's J.P.s had jurisdiction. Eventually the situation was tidied up. In 1404 both Exhall and Foleshill were described in indictments as being in Coventry and its suburbs *(in Coventre et suburbiis ejusdem villa)*, while Styvechale and Whitley were said to be 'in Coventry'[55] .By 1439 the Coventry J.P.s territory was 'the liberty of the town of Coventry'[56] that is, the traditional area of the Cheylesmore leet, soon to become the county of the city of Coventry, a final consolidation of their powers.

Chapter 6: The Jurors

The quarterly session of the peace involved many more Coventrians than the handful of justices. The indictments which the justices would either deal with themselves, or in cases of felony, pass on to a higher court, were presented by either a jury of twelve or thirteen men, or a sworn group of the city's constables, varying from twelve to twenty-nine. In the twenty years from 1377 about ninety men are named as jurors (there must have been more as there are breaks in the records). Over half of them served more than once, a few as many as eight or nine times. There were rather more constables: about a hundred in the five years from 1377. Some men served in both capacities, though not at the same session. Allowing for the missing rolls, an informed guess would put the number involved in the last quarter of the century at about 250. Dr Kimball found that these men represented 'the general run of the middle class population of Coventry'. Of the jurors she said 'in the town the men who are known to have been mayors and masters of the guilds do not seem to have served': of the constables 'The important men did not serve: it was the craftsmen, artisans and tradesmen who were used for police duty'. She also calculated that about two-fifths of the constables and more than half the jurors belonged to the Trinity Guild, so that even if they were not social and economic equals of the mayors who served as J.P.s, they were at any rate their guild brethren.[1] With the advantage of better lists of mayors and bailiffs than Dr Kimball had, we would not dispute her general conclusions, except to say that three men not of mayoral status when they served as jurors did eventually achieve this office: John de Northwode, juror in 1380-81, mayor in 1393; John Cros, juror 1381, mayor 1394: John Barowe, juror 1378, mayor 1404,[2] and that eight jurors, including Northwode and Cros, filled the lower but important office of bailiff.[3] Four constables also became bailiffs,[4] but none became mayor, and this, combined with the smaller proportion who were members of the Trinity Guild, indicates that their social and economic position was, on average, slightly below that of the jurors, while the long interval between being constable and bailiff in some cases, suggests that, as malefactors were often disinclined to 'come quietly', youth rather than experience might be useful in a constable. But they were not all young men.

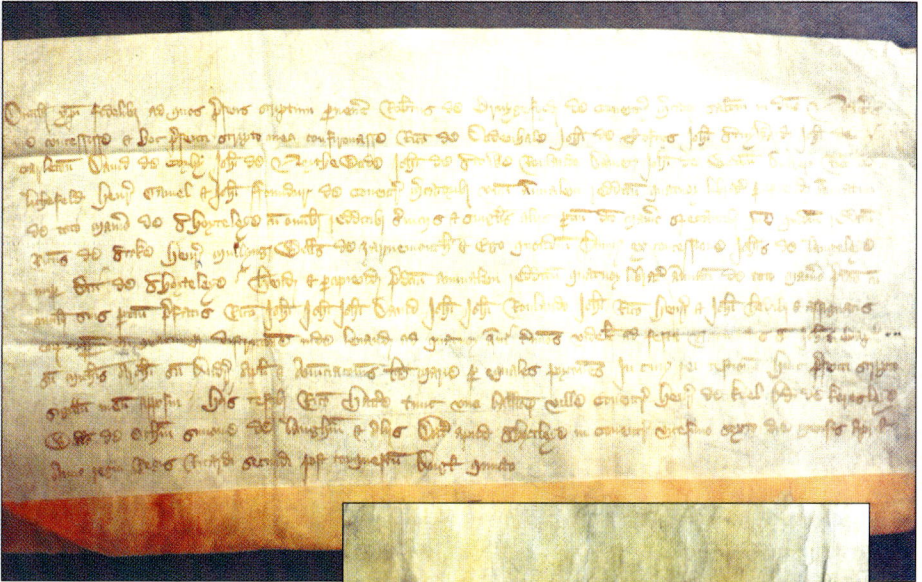

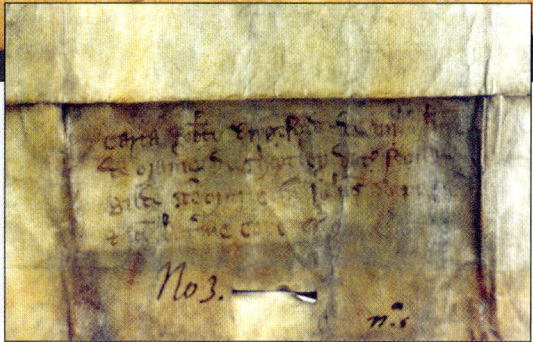

1382 Grant given the seal of St Mary, St John the Baptist and St Katherine as the Trinity Guild with inset of the Endorsement.

This document is given the seal of St Mary's, St John the Baptist and St Katherine's as the Trinity Guild (the union of the 3 was officially confirmed in 1392). It is a grant of 26 April 1382 by Robert de Bruygeford' (of Coventry, merchant) to Richard de Dodenhale, John de Toftes, John Styward', John de Carleton', David de Corby, John de Northewode, John de Stowe, Roland Damet, John de Wedon' (dubber), Richard de Lichefeld', Henry Gamel and John Founder (of Coventry, merchants) of £4 per annum rent as they are the trustees of the Guild. The inset shows the Endorsement of sealing with Trinity Guild seal. It can be surmised that this document had just one wax seal, which was lost possibly in the early 19th Century. The 'No 3' on the endorsement inset relates to early numbering of records by Coventry's Council for part of their case to defend their own power against attempts by central government to gain more power during the early 17th Century.
Reproduced courtesy of Coventry Archives.

Mere wage-earners did not qualify for office: while twenty jurors or constables are identified as traders of some sort by convictions for overcharging, forestalling and regrating, using unauthorised measures or supplying faulty materials,[5] none of nearly fifty men accused of taking excess wages[6] held either office.

If some economic status was needed for office, a 'clean record' was not essential. About twenty jurors or constables had been convicted of some offence before they took office. More than half the offences concerned illegal practices by brewers, innkeepers or ostlers selling ale, horse-bread and oats,[7] but there were also assaults, including an attack on a constable and the breaking of his doors and windows by three men, including Thomas Tuttebiry who became constable himself two years later.[8] Even more startlingly, Thomas Boydon, who was guilty of homicide but escaped hanging by obtaining the king's pardon in 1378, appeared three times as a juror in 1380-81.[9]

Chapter 7: The Justices of the Peace in Action.

The quarter sessions' business may be divided into two approximately equal parts: the upholding of the king's peace, and the enforcement of the laws and customs regulating trade and industry.[1] To take the latter first, by 1377, when the Coventry sessions' records begin, the powers of the former justices of labourers had been given to the J.P.s, and these were also charged with the supervision of weights and measures and the suppression of forestalling and regrating. Forestalling was buying up goods before they reached the market so as to control the price, while regrating was buying goods to sell again at or near the same place at a higher price. The two practices were linked, and both the town officials and the justices fought an ineffective battle against them. People described as 'common' forestallers or regraters (that is, in the habit of doing it) were fined in batches, some of them several times, but the practices continued. Probably, as with Sunday trading until recently, the profits exceeded the fines. Regrating of fish in particular was prevalent, the most notable example being William de Stalworth's meeting early in the morning with fishermen from Chester and Liverpool to buy from them three horse-loads of fish to sell in the town.[2] Other dealers regrated poultry, cheese, butter, fruit, or 'all kinds of food' *(omnibus victualibus).*[3] The number of women fined indicates their considerable involvement in the retail food trade. Attempts to stop the practice met with resistance. John de Clifford, one of the bailiffs attempting to do his duty, was assaulted by an ex-mayor, James Benyngton, supporting the regrators, who were his tenants,[5] and as we have seen, the regrators persisted.[6]

Obviously the authorities had to resist attempts to establish monopolies which held consumers or other traders to ransom, like Ralph Couper's cornering of the market in wine casks, or John Ashbrenner's arrangement with a namesake at Astley in north Warwickshire to buy the whole of his production of the wood-ash used for soap-making.[7] But Robert Fisher's wife, Agnes, who was a 'common regrater' of fresh fish at Spicerstoke, and the thirteen male fish regrators presented at the same court[8] can hardly have been monopolists, and probably linked fisherman to housewife like a modern fishmonger. Medieval legislators, however, were reluctant to allow such middlemen their profit.

The justices attempted to enforce the sale of ale in standard measures, which were supposed to bear an official seal as a guarantee of accuracy. No doubt a fee was charged for sealing, which some were loth to pay, thus incurring fines by the justices, though the drinkers were not necessarily being cheated. Another practice, punished by both the justices of the peace and the Wolfpitlidyate court leet, was sale by 'cups' or 'bowls'[9] which were not legal standard measures but might be customary, rather like the 'glass' of beer which persisted in some districts until the 1930s. Though presumably acceptable to the drinkers, they brought fines on the innkeepers, some of whom were also in trouble for overcharging or giving short weight when supplying oats and horse bread for their customers' mounts.[10] But the justices were not concerned with the bread supplied to humans, for jurisdiction over the bakers remained with the mayor and bailiffs. In other cases, however, they could concern themselves with quality as well as measurement, and the constables presented a tanner who sold defective leather.[11]

We have already observed the justices using their powers under the labour laws to punish employees raising their wages above the statutory rate. One, Alice, a former servant of Adam Walker, not only got sixpence a week, but refused to be hired 'by the year, the half year nor the quarter, but only by the week.' Such exploitation of her talents, whatever they were, led to her indictment before the justices, though we do not know what action they took.[12] Having once been hired for a term it was an offence to leave before the end of it: John Ostiller worked for Margaret Marchal, and their surnames suggest that Margaret owned a farriery or stables, delegating responsibility to John, who departed before his term was up and without submitting accounts. His case went to the court of the King's Bench, where he failed to appear. If he did not show up eventually he would be outlawed.[13]

A feature of the last quarter of the fourteenth century in Coventry is the emergence of associations of journeymen, sometimes disguised as religious guilds. These early attempts at trade unions are called 'journeymen's guilds' by modern writers, but the quarter sessions jury in 1387 called the tailors' association an ' illegal conventicle' and indicted some of its members who were said to have worn a livery cap or hood to show their membership. In resistance to the authority of the masters of the tailors' craft (that is, 'guild') they aimed at control of the journeymen, claiming that tailors newly arrived in Coventry should not be employed until they had joined the 'conventicle', and threatened the death or mutilation of two who were reluctant to join. Their case was transferred to the King's Bench when it came to Coventry in 1387, and six of the tailors were fined. The time for trade unions was well in the future, and neither this conventicle nor other associations of journeymen in Coventry achieved anything important.[14]

Turning from economic affairs to the justices' primary duty of upholding the king's peace, it is apparent that violence was never far from the surface, ready to erupt, sometimes with fatal outcome. In our incomplete records for twenty years there are indictments for twenty-five homicides (one being in self-defence), four robberies (theft involving violence), and three rapes. These were all felonies, all punishable by death, though the criminal often in fact escaped hanging. But there were also 89 serious assaults, treated as trespasses against the king's peace.[15] Men commonly carried knives and staves, tempers were often short, and quarrels could lead to wounding or death. But some violence was premeditated: Walter Bron, a Coventry hosier, though equipped with bow and arrows, sword and dagger, was ambushed and seriously beaten and wounded by a gang of three who made off with his horse, weapons, money and goods.[16] William Thressher alias Forsmyter, armed with bow and arrows, lay in wait to kill his enemy;[17] John de Lutterworth, shoemaker, waylaid another shoemaker, John de Stoke, in Greyfriars Lane.[18] The victims escaped with their lives, but the ambushes were nonetheless regarded as felonious. Other apparently similar offences were regarded as trespasses, and the assailants got off with fines, including four glovers who waited at night outside the gate of Cheylesmore manor-house to beat up Walter de Eton the park keeper.[19] William Marton of Pontefract, accused of waylaying Thomas Barry and attacking him with a knife, claimed that his master, the skinner John de Cruddeworth, had

The first murder, Cain Kills Abel, c. 1000.
English, Christ Church Canterbury (?) c.1000. MS. Junius 11, p49.
Caedman Genesis.
Reproduced courtesy of the Bodleian Library, University of Oxford.

promised him £20 to kill Barry.[20] Cruddeworth had previously been fined at Wolfpitlidyate for housebreaking and taking horses,[21] but this time the jury acquitted him. He served several times himself as a juror at quarter sessions, but another of those he employed in his insalubrious trade, John Wenlok, was indicted in 1380 for stealing a pair of sheets, a carpet, a tablecloth, eighteen lambskins and six rabbit-skins from three separate people.[22] The jurors presented in some detail the case of William Shustoke the younger, who on the evening of Ascension Day 1397 (31st May), was due to surrender himself to face trial the next day. But he was said to have been attacked and seriously beaten in Spon Street by four weavers, armed with swords and cudgels. A rescue party of neighbours took him to safety in Thomas Dyster's house, from where he went next morning to prison, no doubt much to the relief of his surety who had been detained when William failed to appear. The jurors' presentation of this incident is of unusual length and very circumstantial, but when the King's Bench came to Coventry in 1397 and took over the case, the assailants were acquitted.[23]

In the circumstances it is not surprising that the lot of those who had to police the city was often 'not a happy one.' The mayor, bailiffs, sub-bailiffs and constables had authority to arrest offenders or attach their persons or goods to secure their appearance in court. But the accused often resisted, or broke arrest. We have seen already how one constable had his doors and windows broken, and a bailiff punishing regraters was attacked by an ex-mayor.[24] Edward from Ireland, a leech, rebelliously absconded after being arrested by the sub-bailiff.[25] John de Nuby, another sub-bailiff, was beaten and wounded by John Purcere and Lucy his wife, and, on another occasion, attempting to take Richard Sutton's cloak in distraint to compel him to answer John de Oxenford in the mayor and bailiffs' court, was assaulted by Sutton's wife.[26] William Russell, having been arrested by the mayor, made off with a horse which had been put in the constable's charge.[27] In 1396 the night watch were beaten up by a gang of four.[28] These are only some of the instances of attacks on, or resistance to, officials.[29]

Much more serious was the organised rising in 1395 against the mayor, Richard Lichfield, which seems to have been an attempt to take over the city by force. The most notable figure involved was

Sir William Bagot, whose retainers had been accused the year before of intimidating the sheriff of Warwickshire.[30] Bagot himself was a retainer of both John of Gaunt and Richard II, and was rising in the King's favour.[31] Richard had made him steward of Cheylesmore,[32] and his recent acquisition of the manor of Baginton[33] made him a near neighbour of the Coventrians, some of whom supported, or perhaps incited, the rising. Their leader seems to have been the shoemaker, John York, and Robert Shipley, who was to be mayor seven years later, was involved in the plot. The conspirators met on September 7th in Thomas Boteler's house, and next day a hundred armed men appeared on opposite sides of the city intending to beseige it. Probably many were Bagot's retainers, as there were men from Lichfield and Birmingham among them. Presumably the rising failed, but York continued to make trouble until the following May. He and eleven others were indicted before the justices, but Bagot was given separate and favourable treatment, merely being required to appear at Banbury before a special commission empowered to impose a settlement of the quarrel between him and the Coventry authorities. Most of the other insurgents were acquitted by the King's Bench when it came to Coventry. It is difficult to believe in their innocence, as the presentments of four separate groups of jurors and constables cannot have been complete fabrications, but probably Bagot used his influence in the interest of his accomplices.[34]

After violence, the justices were most concerned with theft or larceny. Grand larceny, the theft of property worth more than twelve pence, was a felony, and after indictment before the J.P.s, suspects were tried before the justices of gaol delivery and if found guilty, sentenced to be hanged - the penalty imposed on John Brodoke and the Irishman John Boye for stealing the cloaks of two worthy citizens from the Prior's Hall on a Sunday night.[35] Smaller thefts were petty larceny and the thief was merely whipped and put in the pillory. In addition to the four robberies already mentioned, there were 66 indictments for grand larceny, two for burglary (also a felony) and nine for petty larceny.

Moving from felonies to the less serious charges of trespass against the peace, there were fourteen cases of breaking-in, usually followed by assaults or taking of goods or both, and ten cases of

Selection of Coins from the 13th and 14th Centuries, No.3 has been clipped. All the items were discovered during archaelogical investigation in Coventry. *Reproduced courtesy of the Herbert Art Gallery and Museum, Coventry.*

1) Edward III Groat 1354-5, double shruck   2) 1/2 Groat Edward III,London
3) Silver Farthing Edward I, clipped, London Mint   4) Penny, London
5) Edward III Groat, 1352-3   6) Edward I "Civitras London"

'taking' or 'driving away'.[36] These cases may have covered people making off with goods or animals whose ownership was disputed, but probably most were petty thefts where it was considered that a fine rather than corporal punishment would be sufficient. Thus Joan de Evesham, who 'took' three pennyworth of coal, and William Glover's wife, another Joan, who 'took' a twopenny hen, were fined,[37] but William Workman's wife Isabel, notorious as a common thief, was said to have 'feloniously stolen' fourpennyworth of yarn and a twopenny skillet, and so was due for a whipping.[38]

Several people were designated common thieves,[39] one of them being the Richard de Sutton,' whose wife Maud assaulted the sub-bailiff John de Nuby. The Suttons, with their daughter Agnes, their servant Nicholas and William their associate, were catholic in their tastes for other people's property: between them they stole, from several people, woollen cloth, money, silver, a cup worth 20s, a black horse out of Cheylesmore Park and half a quarter of malt. The malt belonged to John Toftes, an ex-mayor, and a regular justice of the peace, who, however, refrained from sitting when the Sutton gang were indicted. Richard Sutton died before his trial in the King's Bench but Maud and Agnes bought pardons and escaped punishment.[40]

Violence, stealing and breaches of the labour and trading laws occupied most of the justices' time. Of the miscellaneous offences occurring more rarely, three groups call for comment. First, currency offences: obviously a busy trading town such as Coventry, with its markets, inns and much coming and going of strangers, would be an ideal environment for passing forged coins, and it was not only before the justices that such offenders appear.[41] John Marchaunt from Crewkerne in Somerset, and John Russells, were indicted for passing five forged groats (*quinque grossos false monete*),[42] and two chapmen brought £10 worth of Scottish pennies and halfpennies (only three-quarters the weight of English equivalents) to buy from unsuspecting traders.[43] But John Somenour, a coin-clipper, was a Coventrian. The practice of clipping small slivers of gold or silver from coins, which continued to circulate at their face value, thwarted governments' attempts to maintain a sound currency, until the introduction of the milled-edge coins in the seventeenth century. Somenour had been clipping nobles and groats for some time before he was arrested in 1385, when 13s 4d worth of clippings were found at his house. Making or passing false money was high treason, and clipping was felony. We do not know the fate of Marchaunt and Russell or the chapmen, but Somenour, who was tried in the King's Bench, escaped hanging by buying a pardon.[44] Another capital offence was hanging over him though he had not yet been tried. Four years earlier he had gone with about twenty armed men to Warwick, where Nicholas Walker, a Warwick clerk, was held in St Mary's church after conviction for the robbery and murder of John de Clifford, a prominent Coventrian and former bailiff. Somenour and his gang entered the church, seized Walker, beheaded him on a trestle and took his head away with them. When Somenour eventually came up for trial in the King's Bench, he produced another pardon and again went free.[45]

Walker, convicted of murder, had pleaded his clergy and been handed over to the church for punishment. While clerks' lives were thus protected when they committed felonies, in the fourteenth century they could be dealt with in the same way as laymen for lesser offences, and in 1380 three clergy were fined by Coventry J.P.s for extortion: the dean of Coventry, Richard Sadler had got five shillings out of John Canley; the parson of Withybrook, who was the bishop's official, was fined for three separate extortions, one of 26s 8d for the probate of a will. The bishop's sequestrator also extorted too much for probate, some of it in kind, for example, a blanket worth 6s 8d.[46]

Finally the night wanderers. The justices could hardly have envisaged that one day authority would be attempting to revive night-life in the city centre. People about at night were suspect, sometimes rightly so, for Robert Flesshewer and Richard Cook took advantage of darkness to cut down other people's trees,[47] and the constables, watchmen, or whoever it was who at midnight encountered John Grene and Gregory Taillour with drawn swords and drawn bows and arrows[48] had 'reasonable grounds for suspicion', but others merely wandered at night 'against the peace.' Among them was broken-down (decrepitus) Robert Herthull who was dead before any action could be taken against him.[49]

Any narrative based on extracts from court records is in danger of giving an impression of a lawless and violent community, as our selection of a few cases from the rolls of the justices of the peace certainly does. But was fourteenth century Coventry more violent than the city in the 1980s, when the government is again much concerned with law and order? The population of the city in the last quarter of the fourteenth century is unlikely to have exceeded 7,500[50] and the records of the J.P.s' sessions cover the equivalent of twelve full years, in which there were twenty-five homicides.[51] A comparable rate for the present population of the Coventry police division of 310,000 would be over 80 murders or manslaughters a year. In 1988 there were actually three murders and two cases of causing death by reckless driving.[52] Even if the three attempted murders had resulted in deaths, the killings would have been only a tenth of the fourteenth century rate.

But for violence short of homicide our own times are much worse than the late fourteenth century. In the twelve years there were on average eight cases of assault, robbery or rape; a comparable annual rate for the present Coventry division would be about 330 offences. In fact in 1988 there were 789 detected woundings, robberies, assaults with intent to rob, or rapes. These figures must be treated with caution: those from the fourteenth century refer to cases serious enough to warrant a prosecution before the J.P.s and where there was a known suspect to prosecute. We do not know whether some of the accusations were proved, how many offences were committed by persons unknown, how many were ignored or alternatively led merely to claims for damages in the town court or the Cheylesmore courts. On the other hand in 1988 the majority of crimes were cases of wounding, a serious matter at any time; moreover there were a further 370 offences where no suspect was identified. At the least, the figures suggest that the pressure and pace of life in the crowded modern city breeds more violence pro rata than did the bustle of the busy trading and weaving town of the late fourteenth century.

If this is true, why was the homicide rate so much higher? We can only speculate, but two factors come to mind. One, that modern first aid, ambulance and hospital services rescue many victims who in earlier times would have died. Secondly, that when men commonly carried knives and staves, if anger erupted into violence, potentially lethal weapons were to hand. Out of 42 cases extracted from the coroners' rolls,[53] in only seven cases (of ambush, robbery, or attacks by more than one man)[54] is there a presumption of premeditation, not necessarily of murder.

The weapons used in another seven suggest people striking out with whatever they could grab: two people were killed with stones, one by a blow from a spade, another was hit with a small hammer; in self defence a man slew his assailant with a stool; John le Sawier (probably in the timber trade) killed a man with his axe, and in Much Park Street, Thomas Halvemark gave a woman relative a fatal blow on the arm with a poleaxe.[55] Of the remaining 28 homicides, 19 were stabbings with knives, three with daggers, and five men died from blows from staves or cudgels.[56] These were ordinary men's tools or weapons; the remaining case involved the more affluent - a mercer killed a goldsmith with a sword.[57]

But we are more dishonest than our forebears of the fourteenth century. The J.P.s dealt on average with seven cases a year of grand and petty larceny, burglary and 'taking goods' (disregarding the cases of robbery already referred to). In proportion, the number of cases in the Coventry division should be about 290. Actually in 1988 there were over 5,800 detected offences. It is fair to comment that nearly three thousand of these were taking motor vehicles or stealing from them, and that our affluent society provides more property to tempt the dishonest, and, of course, in the twentieth century there is no death penalty for theft, but clearly we are not entitled to be censorious of the morality of medieval Coventrians.

We must also keep in mind that the records of the J.P.s do not give a complete picture; suspects could also be indicted before the mayor and bailiffs, occasionally at the Wolfpitlidyate view of frankpledge, or in the case of homicides, before the coroner, so that our figures for the fourteenth century will be on the low side. But the justices' court had become the main source of indictments, and the picture given by their rolls is not seriously flawed.

It might be argued that the death penalty for serious thefts proved an effective deterrent, but if the fear of being hanged was in the criminal's mind when softly to steal he stole, it must have been tempered by the knowledge that he had a good chance of escaping punishment; Dr Kimball found that in Coventry and Warwickshire 231 persons were indicted for felony between 1377 and 1397. Nothing further is known about 62 of them and four died before they could be tried. Of the other 165 only thirteen were sentenced to be hanged, sixteen were guilty but obtained pardons, 44 were acquitted and 86 failed to appear in court and were outlawed.[58] But these were the cases where there was at any rate a suspect to be charged. To those who escaped punishment must be added 'persons unknown' and even those sentenced to death were not invariably executed.[59]

For the lesser offences of trespass and breaches of the economic regulations, which the justices were empowered to deal with themselves, the 'conviction rate' was much higher; of those whose fate we know after their indictment, two thirds of those accused of trespass were fined, and only one in twenty economic offenders escaped penalty.[60] Of course people who only faced the prospect of a fine were more likely to remain in Coventry and be brought to court than those facing capital charges, while in the higher courts the high proportion of acquittals, about sixty per cent of those actually tried, suggests that juries were sometimes reluctant to find men guilty of felony. In 1381, for instance, two coiners brought before the justices of gaol delivery after arrest in possession not only of counterfeit coins but also the tools for making them, were acquitted by the jury.[61]

Part 3: Other Courts.

Chapter 8: The Justices of Labourers

'*Quia magna pars populi et maxime operariorum et servientium iam in ista pestilencia est defuncta...*' so runs the royal ordinance of 1349: 'Because a great part of the people and especially of workmen and servants, late died of the pestilence, many seeing the necessity of the masters and great scarcity of servants, will not serve unless they receive excessive wages...' Moreover some would-be employers were ready to entice them away from their masters with better offers before they had served their agreed term.

No-one in authority in the mid-fourteenth century believed in allowing free play to market forces, so two royal ordinances of 1349 and a statute of 1351 (commonly known as the Statute of Labourers) attempted to control the 'malice' and 'greediness' of the workers.[1] The aim was to reduce the wage levels to those current in 1342 to 1346, and maximum day wages for many trades were laid down in the statute of 1351. The prices of artefacts were to be as in 1346, but food prices were to allow a moderate profit to the sellers. Leaving employment before the agreed term of service had expired was to be punished by fine or imprisonment. Workers were required to take an oath twice a year to observe the statutes. Employers or buyers were entitled to a refund of the excess wages or prices, or failing claims from individuals, the excess went to reduce the local share of the subsidy granted by Parliament to finance the war with France, thus giving the wealthy an incentive to enforce the law.

The enforcement of the statute was entrusted to the justices of labourers, who were often, but not always, the same men as the justices of the peace. They met in Coventry from 1351 onwards and fined offenders.[2] Two important documents surviving from their activities reveal much about the situation in the city six to eight years after the Black Death. The justices appointed in 1354 were Hugh de Aston, John de Meryngton, Nicholas Michel, Walter Whitewebbe and Richard Frebern.[3] All except Aston were eminent Coventrians.

The first document[4] is a list of fines imposed on offenders in 1355, for in addition to refunding excess pay, those convicted paid a fine to the king. Besides the names of those fined, the list sometimes gives the name of their employers, or of those who complained about overcharging, and it includes people fined for starting prosecutions and not following them up. Sureties who undertook that complainants would prosecute, or that those convicted would pay their fines, and that defendants would appear, are also listed. But the offences are not specified beyond [for taking] 'excess', except in the case of the landlord of the White Cellar who was fined for breaking the assize of ale (either overcharging or giving short measure).

The second document[5] is a list of those presented (that is, accused) before the justices by the constables or juries from Coventry in 1357. Being in effect a schedule of accusations, it is more informative about what offenders are said to have done. Thus, William Typet left his employment before the end of his term and also took 4d a day wages; Nicholas de Drakeford, carpenter, took wages of 6d a day for seven weeks, double the rate fixed by the statute. Richard le Couper managed to get 8d. Two women, Agnes and Alice, refused to work for less than 30s a year. Margaret Braban, a wool- comber or carder, charged 2d a pound for wool. Others are said to have taken specific amounts in excess, perhaps overcharging for a particular piece of work; Richard le Couper of Gosford took 2s too much while Hugh le Couper took 3s 4d. The refusal in 1357 of forty-five people to take the oath to observe the statute indicates serious resistance to the attempt to control earnings. One refuser, Reginald de Teue, had been getting 5d a day, whereas the statute ordained 3d for skilled men and 1d for their labourers. No wonder he refused to be sworn! He and the other forty-four recusants should have been fined or imprisoned, but we have no way of knowing what actually happened to them.

In spite of this resistance, which may not have endured, once the recusants had to face the justices, the legislation and the powers of the justices to enforce it, seem to have been effective, as none of those fined in 1355 were accused again in 1357. Two, however, who had been accused in 1355, but had escaped fines because the complainants failed to follow up their accusations, were presented again two years later.[6]

The two documents combined name 270 convicted or alleged offenders including 62 women. A hundred others appear as employers, complainants or sureties. A small minority of offenders were persons of some substance, perhaps fined for overcharging for goods rather than demanding higher wages, for instance, Richard de Teynton, an ironmonger[7] and one of the founders of the Holy Cross chantry in Trinity Church,[8] and Thomas de la More who seems to have been associated with him.[9] When they failed to appear in 1355 to answer the charges against them, the justices ordered 12d each to be taken from the profits of their lands, as well as fining their sureties. Half a dozen others can be identified as owners or lessees-for-lives of property in Coventry, and if the Willian Bagot fined in 1355 was the one who had land in Sowe and witnessed William Erneys' settlement of his estates there,[10] he should be grouped with them.

The largest fine, 40d, was imposed on John de Coleshill for taking excess pay. If this was the clerk of that name who witnessed deeds in 1346 and 1349,[11] the justices must have been stretching their powers under the statute to cover the pay of non-manual workers. This would not be surprising, as clerks and chaplains who failed to serve out their contracted term were sometimes prosecuted in the courts at Westminster.[12]

But only about a dozen of the 270 offenders are recorded as owners or tenants of houses, or even witnesses to deeds;[13] 31 offenders however do appear on coroner's juries[14] (which must have been hastily assembled as they usually met on the day a body was found, or the day after), and two appear in the coroners' rolls as victims: Agnes Derby, alias Turnspynner, and Katherine wife of John de Hulle, were both murdered, Agnes by her husband.[15]

Obviously, the two lists reveal a stratum of fourteenth century Coventry society about which we should otherwise have known nothing. There are seven men described as weavers in our lists, whereas only one was found in hundreds of deeds of the same period. Fifty-three offenders have apparently no recognised surnames, not even the temporary ones indicating occupation or place of origin but not passed on to the next generation. They are designated by the names of their employers, as, Alice, Robert de Bruggeford's maid *(ancilla)*, Benedict, servant of John Marshall, or even their spouse's employer: Agnes had no more identity than as the wife of Thomas, who was known as the servant of Richard atte Halle. The term 'servant' was widely used for employee, and one must not assume that people so described were household staff, but the women called *ancilla* in Latin, and, in a town, the men designated as *famulus* probably were.

Only the trades for whose services or products there was competition could force up wages or prices. If we consider which they were we shall have some clues to the economic situation in Coventry in the period after the Black Death. Unfortunately, about sixty offenders are merely designated 'servant', 'workman', or 'lad' *(garcio)*, and failing evidence of their employer's business, they cannot be allocated to a trade. The largest number of those whose occupations are known worked in the building trades: eleven carpenters, with one sawyer who prepared their timbers, three slaters, two tilers and one thatcher. Most houses were timber-framed and no masons were fined in 1355. But four were prosecuted in 1357, perhaps the effect of work having been started on building the Town Wall in 1355. These figures are derived from occupations assigned to individuals in addition to their surnames, that is, cast-iron evidence. Generally, in the fourteenth century, it is unsafe to accept a surname as evidence of occupation, but when we get down to the social level where people often had no surnames, where they do occur they are likely to be descriptive of the individual concerned rather than inherited surnames. We find, for instance, that the payment of the fines of John and Thomas Quarreour was guaranteed by a quarry owner,[16] and that John Glover worked for the glover William de Burton, while his surety Adam le Glover was also surety for John de Keteryng, 'glover'. There are traps in using surnames, of course; Henry le Webbe was a carpenter, not a weaver,[17] for instance, but where there is no contradictory evidence it seems worth adding occupational surnames to the positive descriptions of trades. This way we get an extra sawyer and slater, a plumber for the roofgutters, three more masons and two quarriers to supply their stone, making in all thirty workers from the building trades, in fact 11% of all those fined or

Illustration of Coventry Spon (or Bablake) Street Gatehouse from the east, showing St John's Church in the right of the picture.
From a sketch by Dr Nathaniel Troughton. Spon Street Gate was one of the five principal gates of the wall (the others were New, Greyfriars, Bishop and Gosford Gates). The town wall was probably built primarily as a status symbol, although it did play a semi-defensive role on a few occasions. The wall took nearly 180 years to build, from c. 1355 until 1533-34. PA1/2/33b. *Reproduced courtesy of Coventry Archives.*

accused, but 30% of those occupations we can plausibly infer.[18]

The demand for building workers surely indicates that Coventry had swiftly recovered from the effects of the Black Death, and that its economy was buoyant again. Perhaps some of the 88 men who bought one-rood plots from Queen Isabella in 1348[19] were now building on them.

The known or probable occupations of those outside the building trades who were demanding 'excessive' wages show that the city's chief industry was now the production of cloth. Combining given occupations and significant surnames, we have two carders (or perhaps wool combers), one 'turnspynner', ten weavers, two fullers, a dyer and a 'liourmaker' (a producer of narrow fabrics for bindings or tapes). Then there are the 'tipperes', John de Swarkeston and William de Weston, the latter having two employees. Various accounts of what tippers did are given in dictionaries and glossaries, a favourite one being fitting silver tips to drinking horns. But as we find that a Coventry 'tippere' was fined in 1379 for charging two halfpence above the statutory rate for working a stone of wool[20] we include the four among our textile workers, making twenty in all. But there are three others who are almost certainly textile workers, for the lists reveal the presence in Coventry of immigrants from the Low Countries, the 'Flemish weavers' of the old school history books. In Coventry's case they were not Flemings but Brabanters (from roughly the area centred on Brussels), indicated by 'Braban' either as a surname or as a description of origin in addition to occupation, as William Tonour, Braban, webster, accused of homicide at Newark in 1367.[21] Amongst our twenty textile workers already mentioned we have Margaret Braban, kemster (wool carder or comber), Andre le Braban, webbe, Reginald le Webbe of Little Park Street, Braban, and John Braban,, walker (fuller). But it is a reasonable assumption that other Brabanters accused in 1357 were also textile workers, so if we add Michael and Heremon Braban, and Heremon's lad (garcio), we have twenty-three textile workers fined or accused, of whom seven were aliens.

Other Brabanters appear within the next decade. In May 1363, Margaret La Longe, Braban, was killed by another Braban, Robert

Seulere, and Gerekyn Braban was a juror at the inquest.[22] Next year James Braban was killed in a street brawl, leaving a wife Katherine Braban,[23] and in 1378 John Braban was assaulted although already under arrest.[24] But one should not assume that the Brabanters were more given to violence than their English contemporaries. At that economic level both were likely to be recorded only when they were being prosecuted, and there may well have been other, law-abiding Brabanters in Coventry. But clearly the expansion of the city's textile industry had now begun.

It is not suggested that the Brabanters were capitalist entrepreneurs organising the textile industry. As has been pointed out elsewhere,[25] the immigrants were operatives, no doubt skilled in the best techniques, which when copied by the native Coventrians improved their output. It seems likely that Adam and John Brabson who appear in the last twenty years of the century were descended from a Brabanter. Adam was selling (? and making) cloth in 1397-8;[26] he was a constable and on the quarter sessions jury at least once. John was also a constable, and both were guild members.[27] But otherwise there is no evidence that the immigrants or their offspring prospered enough to become part of the Coventry establishment. Nonetheless the surname Brabon still survives in the city.

Were there immigrants from Flanders as well as Brabant? None appears in the lists of offenders against the labour laws, but a John and Juliana de Flaundres held a messuage in Dog Lane before 1343,[28] while Richard de Flaundres seems to have been joint trustee or at any rate temporary keeper, with Henry Dodenhale, of some guild or chantry property.[29] John, Margaret and Thomas Flandres were guild members in the fourteenth century,[30] and seem, with the others from Flanders to have achieved a better status than the Brabanters, but they have no known links with the textile trades.

The assorted metal-workers from our lists form a group of fourteen: besides the ironmonger Richard de Teynton already mentioned, there were two bladesmiths, three smiths, three wiredrawers, a 'ferrier' (probably a supplier of iron) and his employee, and the three servants of William de Bilney, who, as we know from other records, was a needler.[31] After them come seven with the surname Couper (barrelmaker), which suggests that the liquor trade was buoyant!

As we have seen, one inn-keeper was fined in 1355, but the statute allowed food-sellers a 'reasonable' profit, so no other victuallers were prosecuted that year. In 1357, when the justices were also empowered to investigate weights and measures, both the Prior and the corporation secured royal writs confirming their rights to the assize of bread and ale, so removing cases of false measures and overcharging in these commodities from the justices' purview.[32]

Remarkable is the paucity of identifiable workers in the leather trades. A tanner and his mate *(socius)* were accused in 1357, and John de Bilney, servant of Nicholas le Sadlere, refused the oath. No doubt the five glovers made leather gloves, but there are no shoemakers, skinners or whittawers. It would appear that these craftsmen were unable to raise their pay, perhaps because there were as many of them as were needed, unless they lurk among the forty-odd undifferentiated servants and workmen whom we have been unable to allocate to a trade.

Most of the 62 women listed were employed outside their families, but in 1355 ten couples were fined jointly for either demanding 'excessive' wages or overcharging. Roger de Sulby and his wife Joan were fined 12d for contempt and trespass against the King and William and Joan de Bilney', in plain language, for disobeying the royal ordinance and overcharging the Bilneys. The latter must have appeared in court before the justices of labourers to substantiate their original complaint, encouraged no doubt by the prospect of a refund of the excess paid to the Sulbys. Robert le Thatcher and his wife Joan, along with Katherine atte Hulle, escaped fines because the complainants failed to follow up their accusations and were themselves fined for defaulting. Sulby was a glover, and Thatcher really did thatch, but for the other nine couples fined for taking excess we have only surnames as possible clues to their trades, as Netmaker, Gardyner, Smyth, and two couples called Chapman, a chapman being a pedlar or hawker, of course.

Besides the married couples, we have another family unit - Alice Strynger, her son John, and her daughter Alice, who were jointly fined 6d. The Sulbys had an employee who was fined 6d, John atte

Yate being surety for payment of all three. This was by no means the only instance of both master and man being fined or accused. John Kent, a tiler, was fined 12d and his servant William 6d; William de Lutterworth and his servant Richard de Fillongley had to pay 20d each; John Mason and his servant William, both masons, were presented for taking excess pay in 1357, and there were others. Clearly here we have independent craftsmen or small traders working with the help of their wives or a journeyman.

Employers who were not themselves offenders against the statute are only named as a means of identifying their 'servants', that is, their employees. This, however, was often unnecessary, and so we do not know who many of the offenders worked for. Nevertheless, we can identify fifty employers, evenly divided between 1355 and 1357. Nothing in the records suggests that any in this random sample were great entrepreneurs. William de Bilney who, as we know, was a needler in Gosford Street,[33] had three employees who refused to swear to abide by the statute in 1357. Five other employers had two 'servants' each listed, including John Libert, whose two *garciones* may well have been personal or household staff rather than industrial employees. No-one else had more than one delinquent employee. It could, of course, be argued that these masters had other, more docile, workers, but this would imply they they accepted lower wages than their workmates were known to be getting, which seems unlikely. Men are less easily intimidated in groups than singly, so it seems likely that, if larger enterprises had been common in Coventry, some masters' employees would all have demanded the higher rates obtainable and so appeared in our lists of offenders.

It is not surprising that some of the employers were humble people not a lot better off than their workmen, but it is more remarkable that so few of the city's civic elite are found among our fifty employers. There is no-one who had been or was to be mayor, and of the 36 men who were bailiffs in the two decades after the charter of 1345, only two appear, Robert de Bruggesford, bailiff in 1355-6 and coroner in 1362-4,[34] and the merchant Robert de Langham who had been bailiff twice.[35]

Of similar status was Henry Mollyng, who was Master of the important Guild of St John the Baptist in 1357.[36] Bruggesford, however, appears only as the employer of a maid-servant (*ancilla*) and Mollyng of a *famulus*, both probably household servants. Four others of lesser standing were John de Pountfret, mercer or merchant, who became a trustee of the great guilds' properties in the next decade;[37] Robert le Spencer, a founder of the Holy Cross chantry in Trinity Church and probably a member of the abortive Holy Cross guild;[38] the merchant Richard Belers of Gosford Street, [39]and the mercer Robert Cook.[40] Each had a woman employee described as a 'servant', not *ancilla*.

For a wider view of the city's upper crust we can turn to the list of 88 prominent citizens, mostly merchants, who in June 1348 bought one-rood plots in Cheylesmore from Queen Isabella.[41] The Black Death took toll, but 23 survivors can be traced, and no doubt there were many others who are now unrecorded. But only one, Robert de Langham, can be identified with certainty as an employer in 1355 or 1357.[42]

So a mere eight of the mercantile elite who ruled the city appear amongst our fifty employers. Of course the fifty are only a 'sample', but a random one large enough to give a valid picture of Coventry's industrial life. The reason for the magnates' absence from the lists as employers seems to be that the city was still first a mercantile centre, its government dominated by merchants, especially the great wool dealers, exporters whose prosperity at that time would not depend on supplying the looms in the city whether Brabanter or native. The manufacture of cloth, on the other hand, while we know it had a great future in Coventry, was still in the stage of early promise; in a good year 220 cloths were produced for sale in Warwickshire and Leicesteshire combined. Forty years later, over 3,000 were produced in Coventry.[43]

In an industry which was still the province of the self-employed, or small masters with one or two journeymen or apprentices, it is likely that the dealers in cloth were not yet organising the weavers' trade as employers but simply buying their products for resale. Who were these dealers, then? One naturally thinks first of the drapers, who were active in Coventry in the latter part of the thirteenth century,[44] and of course, eminent in the fifteenth.But they seem to have suffered a decline with the decline of the woollen industry after 1300, for among the 700 Coventrians living in the thirty years before 1357 whose occupations are known, [46]there are only three drapers. One of these died before 1328, and there is no mention of the other two after the Black Death.

But in the same period there are ten mercers and six of them at least survived the plague. Drapers were normally only concerned with cloth, but mercers seem to have traded in a wider range of goods - to have diversified as we say today - to have adapted their trading according to what was profitable, and several are alternatively described as 'merchant'. In 1302, mercers were selling cloths (pannos) as well as silks from their stalls in Earl Street.[47] It seems likely then, that in the decade after the Black Death, more mercers than drapers were dealing in the weavers' cloths. We have already mentioned two mercers, John de Pountfret and Robert Cook among our fifty employers, though we cannot link their two women servants with cloth manufacture.

But there may have been others who dealt in cloth; we must remember the much larger number of Coventry men simply described as merchants.The most eminent of them traded in wool; Richard de Stoke, four times mayor, is known as a wool merchant, but was styled 'mercer' in his early days.[48] The wool merchants, in fact, provided most of the mayors throughout the century, and it is not until the 1390s when, as we have seen, cloth manufacture in the city had expanded to fifteen times what it was in 1355, that the first mercer and draper take office.[49]

We find two members of the establishment among the dissatisfied customers. The Master of St Mary's merchant guild, Thomas de Nassyngton, later to be bailiff and coroner,[50] prosecuted two weavers. One, Giles de Lewe, was fined, but Nassyngton himself was fined for false claim when he lost his case against the immigrant Andre Braban. The other eminent complainant was Robert de Shepeye, one of the well-known family of wool-merchants, and an aulnager in four counties,[51] responsible for enforcing statutory dimensions of cloth and the collection of the tax on it. He complained about a bladesmith, Richard Thatcher, but defaulted when the case came before the justices, and he and his sureties were fined. A dozen others failed to follow up their bills. Perhaps they reached agreement with the defendants out of court. It is possible that the threat of an appearance before the justices was used to get a favourable settlement in what was basically a dispute between small traders. For instance, Richard de Oxenford,[52] a locksmith, started, but dropped a case against Peter Le Ferrier whose name suggests another worker or dealer in iron. Weavers showed they could sue as well as be sued: Henry de Sutton, weaver, dropped his case against Alice le Brochere (probably an embroiderer); another 'webbe', Richard de Rommisbury, carried through his prosecution against William de Lutterworth and his servant Richard de Fillongley.

Outstanding amongst all the complainants was the abbot of Pipewell, who succeeded in getting ten people fined, including six women. No-one else prosecuted so many. The abbot of Coombe started a case against a carpenter, Thomas Trayvill, but let it lapse. Coombe Abbey had several properties in Coventry[53] and the abbey itself was only four miles away, but Pipewell was thirty miles off, and while the monks had an important grange at Cawston, near Dunchurch, and other properties west of Rugby,[54] they had nothing within ten miles of Coventry. The men prosecuted were John Quarreour and his son Thomas (almost certainly quarrymen), Thomas Walker (? a fuller) and Thomas Deyster. We have no means of knowing whether these were workers who had deserted the abbot's service for the attractions of Coventry, or whether the abbey's bailiffs were coming to the city for stone and cloth-finishing workers.

One of the abbot of Coombe's sureties who had undertaken to ensure that he would follow up his complaint against Trayvill, was the mayor, Richard de Stoke, a founder and past master of St John the Baptist's guild.[55] When the abbot dropped his case, his two sureties were jointly fined sixpence. Stokes could regard such a penalty as trivial for he was a great merchant and exporter of wool, including the abbot's.[56] His associate in wool dealing, Richard Buttere, a future bailiff and trustee of St Mary's Hall[57] had to pay his half share of a fourpenny fine when John Child, for whom he had stood surety, also failed to proceed against William Haithale.

Sureties, generally known as pledges or mainpernors, were an essential part of medieval justice and administration. In 1355 we have over 70 people named as pledges, most of them for payment of fines but some supporting prosecution or defence. Among them were seven who were at some time bailiffs,[58] including the wealthy merchant John Prest, a founder of Corpus Christ guild,[59] who had been a mainpernor for a defaulting defendant, Thomas de la More. There was also another of the founders of St John's guild, Peter de Stoke,[60] its future master Henry Mollyng,[61] and Laurence de Northfolk, one of 'The Twelve' who purchased the city's privileges from Queen Isabella in 1345.[62] Several of these worthies were sureties for quite humble people. Northfolk, for instance, guaranteed that Alice, servant of the mercer John Pountfret, would pay her sixpence fine, and John de Bricstoke, bailiff in 1355,[63] did the same for another Alice, maidservant of his successor Robert de Bruggeford.[64] Another former bailiff and merchant, Walter de Stoke,[65] was surety for the fines of a tiler and his man. Whatever the relationship between these magnates and the offenders, patronage, charity or just friendliness, it bridged a considerable economic and presumably social gap. The landlord of the White Cellar (at the corner of Earl Street and Much Park Street) turned for his surety to the merchant Henry Dilcok, who had been chamberlain and was soon to be bailiff.[66] Perhaps Dilcok drank in his tavern!

Nine employers were sureties for their workers. It must not be assumed that the complaint about excess pay was necessarily made by the employer, who may have been happy to pay the market rate until it came to the ears of a constable or juror. However, if an employer had succeeded in forcing down an employee's wages by complaining to the justices, he would have gained nothing if the servant lay in gaol for want of a surety.

In other cases the economic relationship between offender and surety was a more equal one. People turned to those they were accustomed to do business with. Andrew le Follere was surety for the weaver Giles de Lewe; Henry de Sutton, another weaver, for Joan Kembster (wool comber or carder) and Hugh le Webbe for Thomas Walker (probably a fuller). Hugh owned the site of Viel's quarry,[67] and was pledge for John Quarreour and his son Thomas.

Seven offenders who were fined and produced sureties for payment were themselves sureties for other offenders. Over eighty years ago Bertha H. Putnam commented on this practice, and suggested that the security system had become a mere formality, perhaps because there were not enough gaols to hold offenders.[68] She assumes that those fined did not pay on the spot because they were unable to find the money, but that was not necessarily the reason. The process of collection by the sheriff of fines imposed by the justices was slow and sometimes uncertain, so why should anyone pay then when he had the option of paying later? Particularly as, in the case of Coventry at any rate, it could be several years later. Those fined in 1355 would know that the fines imposed in the previous four years had still not been collected, and they were still unpaid, along with those for 1355 and 1356, in 1359, as the sheriff of Warwickshire had not had entry into the liberty of Coventry to collect them, probably because the corporation were themselves laying claim to the fines.[69]

Obviously we cannot assume that those who found sureties for payment were not acceptable as guarantors themselves, and the appearance of eminent merchants standing for humble maidservants with no surname suggests that the practice was no mere charade. Failing friends, business links or patrons, it seems that one could turn to a few people who made a speciality of providing security, perhaps for a fee like the present-day bondsmen in the United States. Richard Belers, a merchant,[70] either alone, or with another surety, guaranteed the fines of ten people including his own servant Isabel. It is perhaps just credible that the other nine were friends or business connections, but William de Burton, a glover, was surety for fifteen offenders and two prosecutors, while Robert de Lapworth guaranteed the fines of 21 offenders. We know almost nothing about Lapworth. He appears in 1348 as a former owner of a tenement in Well Street, and his position as last of the witnesses to a deed in 1359[71] suggests that he might have been a clerk, as Robert de Everdon, who was pledge for five offenders and one complainant, certainly was.[72] John atte Gate was surety for eight fined by the justices of labourers and five by the justices of the peace in 1355.[73] In 1360 he was mainpernor for Richard Darker's appearance before the justices of gaol delivery, and later stood for his fine and subsequent good behaviour,[74] and in

1361 was pledge for a prosecution in Cheylesmore manor court.[75] Presumably he was some sort of legal agent, and Lapworth may have been the same.

A study of the sureties in 1355 has revealed something of the connections which could exist between Coventrians of all levels of wealth and civic importance. The categories into which we have divided those people named in 1355 are to some extent artificial. Employers could be offenders, and either could be sureties. Employers could be little above the wage-earner level. Some employers and sureties are well-documented, others, like most of the offenders, are unrecorded except in this one document. The links between individuals, economic, social, co-operative or exploitative, were part of the web which formed the social fabric of the city.

Over 270 offenders, employers, complainants or sureties, are named in the list of 1355. There were others involved in the sessions who were not listed; constables, jurors, clerks, perhaps 300 people in all. The list probably covers three of the justices' quarterly sessions, so about one hundred people would be involved when the justices were in session. Beforehand, there would be the tendering of the oaths to observe the Statute of Labourers; unfortunately we have no record of those who took the oath, only the refusers. No doubt the sessions caused quite a stir in the city!

After 1359 there were no separate justices of labourers, and offences against the labour laws were dealt with by the justices of the peace in ordinary quarter sessions. We have no record of these before 1377. Presumably by then the balance between employers and workers, so drastically tilted by the Black Death, had to some degree levelled out, as there were only 39 prosecutions in the next three years, but 31 of these were at the quarter sessions of 12 July 1379. Of these defendants, nine were either described as 'wright' (carpenter) or surnamed Wright.

Obviously Coventry's building boom continued, and an attack was being made on carpenters' earnings. In January 1380 it was the turn of the shoemakers, who provided five of the six offenders;[76] it will be recalled that there were none in 1355 or 1357. Thus, while

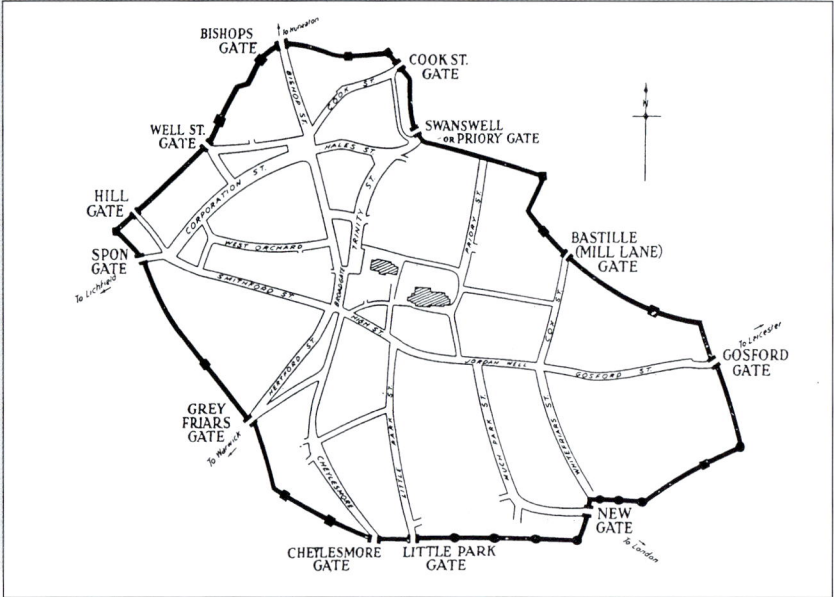

Plan showing the line of Coventry city wall and gate in relation to the street plan of central Coventry c.1945.
Taken from 'Coventry's Heritage' by Levi Fox, 1947.

Illustration of a City Wall, Mid 14th Century. Similar to that of Coventry. MS Auct. D.4,17, fol.20v.Apocalypse, English, Mid 14th Century.
Reproduced courtesy of the Bodleian Library, University of Oxford.

there was no longer the spate of prosecutions of the 1350s, employers or the authorities were still determined to try to prevent the artisans from exploiting their economic advantage. Looking forward a little, however, it is clear that they could not hold back the tide indefinitely. The men working on the town wall were perhaps in a favourable position because it was advancing so slowly, but in 1393 there is record of seven masons working for $4\frac{1}{2}$d a day instead of the statutory 3d, and two years later they actually received a rise of $4\frac{1}{2}$d extra, while their labourers were getting 3d a day, twice the amount laid down for them by the statute.[77]

Aggrieved employers could resort to other courts. The original ordinance of 1349 had envisaged prosecutions in the manorial courts, and in 1365 Ranulph Emmote tried to use the Cheylesmore manor court to compel a girl who had left his service before the end of her term to return to him. However, he dropped the case perhaps because by the time the court met, her term (from Michaelmas to Lady Day) had only a month to run.[78] John Martyn of Combrook, who broke his contract with William de Kyngeston of Coventry did not escape so lightly. In 1378 Kyngeston sued in the Court of Common pleas at Westminster. As the sheriff of Warwickshire failed to find Martyn to produce him in court, he caused, him to be outlawed. Martyn later surrendered to the court and was imprisoned in the Flete.[79]

Illustration of a Dyer, c. 1320-30.
Christ was said to have been apprenticed to a dyer. MS. Seldon supra 38g fol. 27. Apocryphal Childhood of Christ, English, c.1320-30. *Reproduced courtesy of the Bodleian Library, University of Oxford.*

Illustration showing Merchants watching cargoes arrive, Mid 14th Century. MS. Bodley 401, fol.55v. apocalypse English, Mid 14th Century. *Reproduced courtesy of the Bodleian Library, University of Oxford.*

Chapter 9: Cheylesmore Courts

[Introduction (Trevor John):

This final chapter deals with the remaining local courts which exercised jurisdiction over fourteenth century Coventrians and were sometimes used by them to try to obtain justice. The records of most of the several courts within the city controlled by the corporation have not survived. However, as has been seen in previous chapters, the coroners' rolls record some cases, particularly those where accident or violence resulted in death, or when accusations (appeals) were made by criminals against their accomplices in order to save their own skins. The proceedings before the justices of the peace reveal Coventrians prosecuted for assault, petty theft, the infringement of the Statute of Labourers and breaking regulations controlling the markets and the price of commodities.

Some further cases involving the citizens are to be found in the rolls of the manorial court (the court baron) of Cheylesmore manor which included villages and hamlets surrounding the city. This is because some Coventrians held property outside the city, as for example Richard Frebern, bailiff of Coventry in 1349, who had an estate in Whitley, and were thus obligated to attend the court held every three weeks at Cheylesmore (see p83 and p84). Owing 'suit of court' as it was called, was a normal condition of holding property on a manorial estate. Linked with the Cheylesmore court was the twice yearly court leet (or view of frankpledge) meeting at Wolfpitlidyate, which dealt with offences against law and order and 'nuisances' such as blocked ditches and badly maintained highways. These courts were normally presided over by the Black Prince's steward. The court leet had not been transferred to the city's administration as it should have been according to the Tripartite Indenture of 1355. Why this had not been done is not known.

A broken, incomplete series of Cheylesmore court rolls begins on 1st February 1360. Non-attenders, great or small, were fined. Tenants had to render homage and fealty (see p84) to the prince for their lands. When one of them died and his heir was under age, the heir became the ward of the prince, and his land was taken over by the prince's administration which would take the profits from it and also might sell the marriage of the heir. In this way the marriage of Thomas, grandson and heir of Richard Frebern, was sold to Richard de Sutton for ten marks (£6 13s 4d.)

Actions concerning for example trespasses (then almost any unlawful act other than treason or felony) or pleas of debt could be brought before these courts by individuals who were not necessarily tenants of the manor. And this applies to the defendants in some cases too. Defendants could delay proceedings against them by simply not turning up when summoned, though eventually they risked the court 'distraining' them (that is seizing some of their goods and chattels) to compel attendance. The abbot of Coombe seems to have been particularly reluctant to meet his creditors and adept at avoiding them (see pages 86-87 and 91).

The Cheyslemore court was useful to locals in pleas of debt. Sometimes citizens would pursue a debt there in preference to the city portmanmoot, though officially they ought not to have done so. Their hope must have been for quicker or more favourable justice in the prince's court. Additionally the central royal court, the Court of the Common Pleas at Westminster, would not entertain pleas where the value of goods, debts or damages was less then 40s. Also the fees and expenses involved in a plea at Westminster were high, and inevitably this would favour the richer of the two parties involved. Thus Cheylesmore was a convenient court for Coventrians where small debts of under 40s were involved, and where the defendant was more rich and powerful than the plaintiff and could afford the expense and delays of the central court. Indeed Agnes de Pakynton, probably acting as the executor of her husband's will for a debt of over £8 owed him by the abbot of Coombe, sued the abbott for five debts of 39s 11d or less simultaneously in order to stop the wily abbot from having the case removed to the Court of Common Pleas (see p XXX). Unfortunately, because of the incompleteness of the court's records, it is not known whether this brought her any more satisfaction than the abbot's other creditors.

Collection of reproductions of the seals of Coventry, 14th Century.

1) Impression of the earliest Common Seal, the seal of the community of the Ville of Coventry. The Corporation of the Mayor, Bailiffs and Commonalty was created by the charter of 1345. a) Obverse b) Reverse

2) Impression of the Statute Merchant Seal. Authority to take cases of debt and use the Statute Merchant Seal was granted by the charter of 1345. Obverse. *Reproduced courtesy of Coventry Archives.*

More detail of these and other cases in which medieval Coventrians reveal their litigious and often cunning nature is to be found in the text which follows.]

As we have seen, after the charters of 1345-46 the corporation controlled several courts with jurisdiction within the city, and, in the case of the Court of the Liberty, in the villages and hamlets subordinate to the manor of Cheylesmore. Before these courts would come disputes between citizens: actions for small debts; the multifarious wrongs which in the fourteenth century were comprised under 'trespass'; disputes over contracts and the ownership of goods. The 'fines' whereby conveyances of houses and land were secured and recorded, were 'levied' before the mayor and bailiffs in the Court of the Liberty. Historians of towns where the records of such courts have survived have used them to build up lively accounts of the daily life and work of the citizens.

For Coventry, alas, the records of the corporation's courts and the Prior's court in his own half have not survived. The coroners' rolls record cases where accident or violence resulted in death, and the 'appeals' where criminals accused their accomplices to save themselves.[1] After 1377 the records of the justices of the peace reveal some of the delinquencies of the Coventrians, with the prosecutions for assault, petty theft, infringements of the statute of labourers, or of the regulations controlling the marketing and prices of provisions.[2] But ordinary disputes between citizens which could not be construed as breaches of the king's peace or of statutes did not come before the justices. We can, however, find some such cases involving Coventrians in the rolls of the court baron of Cheylesmore manor, beginning shortly after the death of Queen Isabella.

When Isabella died in 1358, her grandson the Black Prince succeeded to Cheylesmore, and the Queen's interests in the Coventry area. Sir Hugh de Hopwas was despatched on August 28th to secure possession. On September 20th, the Prince's council met at Cheylesmore, when John de Pakynton, a Coventrian, was appointed steward, with authority to hold the 'foreign courts' of the manor.[3] 'Foreign' meant outside the city, including places immediately adjoining, like Radford, Harnall, Spon, Whoberley,

Stoke and Whitley, as well as more distant villages and hamlets now absorbed into the modern city. As many Coventrians had property in these areas, they owed suit, that is, had an obligation to attend the Prince's courts. Their position had been regulated in the Tripartite Indenture of 1355, where it was made clear that only those citizens who had land outside the town need attend Isabella's three-weekly court at Cheylesmore. This was the court baron in our terminology, though never so called in its records, where it is termed 'the little court', or just 'court'.

Linked with this court, but held at six-monthly intervals, was the court leet, or view of frankpledge as it was invariably called. This met at Wolfpitlidyate, and was concerned with law and order, and nuisances such as blocked watercourses and impassable highways. According to the Tripartite Indenture, Isabella's rights over this court were to be transferred to the corporation, but for some reason unknown to us, the Queen retained them, and they passed to the Black Prince.[4] These were the courts which Pakynton was to hold, but his tenure of the stewardship was short, for within three months Sir Richard de Stafford was appointed keeper of the manor; he was, however, allowed a deputy to do the work for him, who may, of course, have been Pakynton. In September 1359, perhaps because Pakynton had died, de Stafford appointed Henry del Stanydelf to hold the courts for a salary of sixty shillings a year,[5] and Stanydelf was described as steward in 1366.[6]

Although the courts were long-established, no records of their proceedings before Isabella's death have survived, so we cannot compare the Black Prince's lordship with hers, but a broken series of court rolls begins on 1st February 1360,[7] when we can see that the officials have settled in, and are asserting the Prince's rights.

Cheylesmore, originally the estate of the great earls of Chester, was more than an ordinary manor, and the three-weeks court more important than the courts baron of small lords. Several of the tenants who owed suit at the court were themselves lords of villages in the Prince's 'foreign'. Two, John de Botiler of Exhall, and John de Mowbray of Caludon, were knights.[8] Isabel Stowell, lady of Keresley, was supposed to attend the three-weekly court at Cheylesmore and the twice-a-year court at Wolfpitlidyate, and when the former mayor of Coventry, Henry le Clerk, acquired her property, he was summoned to appear to show his title deed, and be bound to do the same suit.[9]

In the early years of the Black Prince's lordship, the lords of Ansty, Caludon, Stoke, Foleshill, Exhall, Asthill (where no-one lived, but the duke of Lancaster was lord), and Tackley (in Oxfordshire, forty miles away), were required to attend and acknowledge the Prince's overlordship. Mostly they defaulted and were fined small sums, sixpence or less.[10] But the prince's rights were not trivial, as some, perhaps most, of these tenants held their property by 'knight service'; under this tenure, if the heirs succeeded as minors, they became wards of the Prince, who held their estates till they came of age, and had the right to arrange their marriage. One eminent Coventrian subject to these onerous conditions was Richard Frebern, bailiff in the year of the Black Death, whose family had built up an estate - not yet called a manor - in Whitley. He held by knight service, and was fined for not attending the first court for which we have the record.[11] In 1364 this estate was in the Black Prince's hands during the minority of Richard's grandson Thomas, and the keeping of the lands, of Thomas himself, and the right to arrange his marriage, was sold for ten marks to Richard de Sutton, perhaps a relative or friend of the Freberns.[12] Another Coventrian fined at the same court for not doing suit was the skinner Richard le Darker, a founder of St Katherine's guild, and, at his death in 1374, holder of the manor of Whoberley.[13]

As well as these lords of dependent manors, over thirty other people were warned to attend at Cheylesmore to do homage and fealty to the Prince, some of them eminent, including three who were at some time coroners, though an old suit roll must have been used as it seems certain that several of them were dead. Most of the others, like their social superiors, did not respond first time, and the process was repeated at several courts.[14] Presumably they eventually did what was required, but there is a gap in the court rolls. Those who were unable to travel might be visited by an official called the Keeper of the Prince's fees.[15] It must not be assumed that all these people held land outside the town. While the Tripartite Indenture ruled that Isabella's tenants holding only within the town were exempt from the three-weeks court, there is no suggestion that they were excused fealty, that is, taking an oath to be true to the lord, and faithfully perform the services due (which by this time meant pay the customary rent and attend the courts). In fact, in 1361, Thomas de Stonley was required to do fealty for half a burgage in the town which he had acquired by marriage to an heiress.[16]

Obviously fealty must be performed when there was a new lord, or a new tenant. Regular attendance at the court every three weeks was another matter, and it was becoming customary for some tenants to pay fines for absence regularly rather than appear. In 1364 John de Denecourt and Richard le Darker paid fines in advance to cover their absences for six months and a year respectively.[17] Ten years later, Darker and six others, including John Nowers, lord of Tackley, paid fines, probably for a period. At the same court, on Lady Day, attempts were being made to secure the attendance - or fines in lieu, presumably - of eighteen other people, including the Prior of Coventry, Sir Baldwin de Freville (one of the Prince's retainers, who had acquired Shortley, Pinley and Wyken), Sir John Peyto, and the Duke of Lancaster (John of Gaunt, the Prince's brother).[18] Obviously Gaunt would not attend in person, but in 1379, for instance, a Coventrian, John Ray, represented him.[19]

It is clear that a review of obligations was under way, and three weeks later, the results were recorded in a list of twenty-four alleged suitors: Lancaster's attendance was respited (that is, a delay was allowed), because he was overseas; de Freville was not liable for service for Pinley; Peyto and his wife Eleanor, who held a manor in Sowe, were to be distrained; the Prior ought to do suit for William Bagot's lands which he had acquired; Darker was dead, and inquiry was to be made into who held his land; William Erneys' former holding in Attoxhall, still known as Erneys Place, was held by Thomas Longhurst, and the abbot of Stoneleigh owed suit for land in Whoberley; the Mowbray heir was under age and a ward of the king. Moreover it was claimed that a deed of the Earl of Chester had discharged the suit due from the lords of Caludon.[20] Eleven of the twentyfour, perhaps more, were citizens of Coventry. Richard Clerk, a future mayor, held the manor of Keresley, and four citizens who at some time were bailiffs also owed suit.[21] The proviso in the Tripartite Indenture, that Coventrians should only do suit if they held land outside the city was clearly being observed.[22]

The steward who was responsible for the courts was not always present: in November 1364, Master John le Flesshewere came to the court to claim his bull, which had been impounded as a stray, but in the absence of the steward, he was not allowed to take it, and the court made arrangements for it to be kept and fed.[23] Presumably the bailiff conducted the court in the steward's absence.

Besides those who owed suit, there were the litigants who came to prosecute, or, reluctantly, to defend themselves. Some were, of course, suitors, but others may not have been. Certainly some were from the city itself rather than the foreign. Joan le Deister of Gosford Bridge,[24] Richard le Deister of Gosford,[25] Roger le Sherman of Much Park Street,[26] John le Poulter of West Orchard,[27] John Hatter of Spon Street,[28] Brother Richard de Downes, Prior of the Carmelites,[29] Henry the Master of St John's Hospital,[30] Richard Butter and Nicholas Scathelok of Coventry,[31] and John le Clerk de Stoneley 'of Coventry',[32] are located by their style in the court rolls, as are others who will be mentioned later. Some we can identify as citizens from references elsewhere.

The litigants maintained a stream of business, sluggishly flowing through the procedural obstructions of medieval litigation, whereby defendants could delay their appearance in court. It has been pointed out that, in the courts conducted by the King's justices at Westminster, over two years and eight months could pass, while the processes of attachment and distraint moved towards the point where the defendant's lands were seized to persuade him to appear in court to answer the plaintiff.[33] At most four steps in the process (one in each law term) could be taken in a year, so rapid progress could not be expected. The Cheylesmore court, on the other hand, met every three weeks, but frequency did not necessarily mean swift satisfaction for the plaintiffs.

A classic example of the way a reluctant and determined defendant could delay judgement is provided by the abbot of Coombe, Robert de Atherstone.[34] The first surviving court roll, of Ist February 1360, records that he is being sued for debt by three separate plaintiffs:

Hugh de Hopwas, one of the Black Prince's retainers, the abbot of Merevale, and the rector of Grendon, Robert de Immingham. It is clear that the cases had opened at an earlier court, as the process of attachment (that is, requiring the defendant to give security for his appearance in court to answer the plaintiff) had reached its second stage - the court ordered the abbot to be attached *sicut pluries* - as often [before]. Three weeks later he was to be attached *sicut alias*[35] - as formerly. This exhausted the process of attachment, and on March 14th the court started the more drastic process of distraint, the taking of some chattel of the defendant into the court's custody until he appeared. The abbot still did not appear, and at the next two courts was ordered to be distrained *sicut pluries*. His persistent lack of response did not exhaust the court's patience (or its vocabulary), and on May 16th begins a series of orders for distraint *sicut plus pluries* - as more often, renewed regularly every three weeks until March 27th 1361, when the order was changed to distraint *sicut alias* in the case of Immingham only. Unless it was a scribal error, this should have indicated some sort of procedural crisis or change in that case at least, but the rolls of the next three courts are damaged or missing, and there is no mention of any of the cases when the records resume on June 18th. But at the next court the familiar names and phrases reappear with orders for distraint *sicut plus pluries*. Eighteen months and at least twenty-six sessions of the court had passed since the three plaintiffs had sued, and the abbot had not yet appeared in court. Strong action was evidently called for, and eight oxen, a bull, three cows and a heifer were 'seized' in distraint. This may at first have been no more than a formal declaration that they were now nominally in the court's custody. Certainly the abbot did not immediately appear, and the court ordered even more drastic (*melius* - better) distraint, perhaps actually depriving the abbot of the use of his animals. At last, on 21 August 1361, the abbot acknowledged his faults of non-appearance, for which he was fined 12d and given a day for trial of the cases between him and his creditors. Even at this stage, defendants could further delay proceedings by essoining, that is, sending someone with an excuse for their non-appearance (theoretically because they were ill), but the court ordered that no essoins be allowed.

The abbot did not essoin himself at the next court, but did not turn up either, and all the court could do was fine his surety, and order 'better' *(melius)* distraint. This process continued until 4th December that year. Unfortunately the rolls of the next ten courts are missing, and when we pick up the record again there is no mention of the three cases. If the three plaintiffs got any satisfaction from the abbot - and it is by no means certain that they did-it had taken them two years and more than thirty courts to get it.[36]

The court rolls resume on July 23rd 1362; by then an even more longdrawn-out suit against the abbot was in progress. Agnes de Pakynton widow and executor of the will of John de Pakynton, the former steward of Cheylesmore, was suing the abbot in five separate pleas of debt. Orders to distrain the abbot's successors continued until January 1366, when a horse worth two marks had been distrained on, and four sureties, one of them the Cheylesmore bailiff, had pledged the abbot's appearance. But he still did not turn up, and the tedious repetition of orders for distraint - punctuated occasionally by the bailiff's report that he could find nothing to distrain on - continued until September, well over four years after Agnes originally sued. Again we are denied the final outcome, as the rolls for a whole year are missing.[37]

But the abbot could resist the court for longer than four years ! Before October 1365, while Agnes was still suing, another creditor appeared, Richard Belers, a merchant of Gosford Street, and life tenant of much, if not all, of William Erneys' former estates centred on Attoxhall in Sowe.[38] The distraint on the abbot's horse in the following January was intended to force him to answer Belers as well as Agnes. But, while Agnes disappears during the year's break in the rolls, when they resume Belers has added a new plea, and he was still suing on the two in September 1374, by which time his action had been entered on the rolls of about a hundred and fifty courts.[39] By that time did anyone expect a result? And is it credible that the bailiff tried so many times to find something to distrain on? Perhaps the case was just carried forward from court to court because it had never been formally terminated. It disappears into the five-year gap in the rolls after 1374, but it seems unlikely that Belers ever got his money.

These long-drawn-out actions, often with no apparent progress, resulted from the reluctance of English courts to judge an absent defendant, even though he had been repeatedly summoned, combined with the limited effectiveness of attachment and distraint in compelling attendance. If nothing of value could be found on the defendant's premises within the court's jurisdiction, distraint was impossible, so cunning defendants hid their property elsewhere. Such a one was Agnes de Ideshale, sued by John Skarlet for trespass, debt and detention of chattels. After more than a year of orders to distrain her, the court learned that her goods were in William de Bilney's house, and the bailiff was ordered to seize them and attach Bilney to answer at the next court, for trespass and contempt. The result is curious. Bilney turned up and eventually pledged that he would defend himself, but Agnes still failed to appear, either immediately or at the next twelve courts.[40]

Other litigants were not prepared to persist so long. Sometimes they agreed by licence of the court, as for instance William in the Hollies, miller of Whitley mill, and the two millers at New Mill whom William had started to prosecute for trespass and detention of chattels.[41] Sometimes the plaintiff dropped the case, paying a fine to the court, otherwise, after distraints and essoins, the point was eventually reached where the defendant must 'do his law', that is, take a solemn oath, supported by the oaths of five others, that he was innocent of whatever the plaintiff alleged against him. Even at this stage some defendants defaulted, probably because they could not get five men to vouch for what they said in front of neighbours who might have a shrewd idea of the truth of the matter. At this point the court would rule that the plaintiff had won his case. The court's patience, or resignation, with defendants was not extended to strangers; John de Walleford of Wolverton, sued for debt, had to pledge his horse and saddle to guarantee his appearance.[42]

It might be surmised that the tedious and lengthy process of pursuing an obstinate adversary, and the court's near impotence viv-a-vis a recalcitrant defendant, would discourage plaintiffs from resorting to Cheylesmore for justice. But in fact, from 1360 to 1374, business increased, whether measured by the number of entries on the rolls, or the money collected. The money came from fines which were levied not only on defaulting defendants but on

Illustration of Cheylesmore Manor Gatehouse, Coventry, in the 19th Century.

The earliest documentary reference to a manor house at Cheylesmore is in 1250, but the park in which it stood can be traced back another century. The Prince was given the right to hold a court leet within the manor and to have a gaol there in the 1345 'Charter of Incorporation'. During Richard II's reign, the 436-acre park, which included woodland, was partly stocked with deer, and in 1385 this royal manor was incorporated within the city walls, then being erected. In 1388, part of the park was separated from the rest and called the 'Little Park'; thereafter, the Great and Little Parks gave their names to Much and Little Parks Streets.

The building that we know today as Cheylesmore Manor House is in fact, only the gatehouse and parts of the two cross wings (north and south) to the original manor house.

Text reproduced courtesy of Heritage Open Days 2000 leaflet on Cheylesmore Manor House.

unsuccessful plaintiffs for 'false claim', plaintiffs who dropped their case, sureties whose principals failed to appear, and so on, plus, of course, the payments in lieu of attendance from those owing suit.[43] If we find it surprising that people continued to use the court, we must consider what alternatives they had. The ancient liberties of the great earls of Chester must have excluded their tenants from the local hundred and county courts which would otherwise have dealt with the kind of cases brought to Cheylesmore.[44] And presumably only those resident, or holding property in the town could resort to the portmoot. These were all parallel rather than superior courts. Could a higher jurisdiction be sought? The Court of Common Pleas at Westminster was the obvious place for those prepared to face the expense. But that court would not enterain pleas where the value of the goods, debts or damages claimed, was under forty shillings, as the majority of the Cheylesmore cases probably were. As we have seen, the charters of 1345 and 1346 had given to the mayor and bailiffs jurisdiction over many cases arising within 'the view of frankpledge of the manor of Cheylesmore', that is, the area subject to the Cheylesmore courts. They exercised this right in the Court of the Liberty, but the vestigial records of this court which have survived are all concerned with real property, either conveyances or disputed titles.[45]

As the charters had granted powers previously belonging to the king's courts, however, presumably the forty-shilling rule would apply, thus excluding most of the Cheylesmore cases. Moreover the jurisdiction of the mayors and bailiffs, though wide-ranging, was limited to the list of pleas specified in the charter, from which actions for debt or detention of chattels are noticeably absent. It is possible, though we have no evidence for it, that such cases were brought before the Court of the Liberty by 'plaint', that is, starting an action by oral or written complaint to the court without having obtained the king's writ, as the charter gave the mayor and bailiffs jurisdiction over all plaints. But for those prepared to pay, the king's courts at Westminster were available for cases of debt and detention involving forty shillings or more, and probably other pleas.

The higher justice did not come cheap, however. The plaintiff must purchase a writ, pay an attorney to manage the case for him, probably for at least four law terms, and quite likely also pay a pleader to argue with the defendant's lawyer in court. Having gone to this expense, the plaintiff might not get a judgment within two and a half years, and wily defendants could extend that time. In fact it was often defendants who had cases removed from local courts to Westminster to cause maximum delay. Agnes de Pakynton's five simultaneous pleas of debt were almost certainly a ploy to prevent this. By dividing her claim into five amounts of 39s 11d or less, she would debar the abbot of Coombe from having the case removed to the Court of Common Pleas, a device which was certainly employed elsewhere.[46] Swift judgment of an obstructive defendant was not to be had in the fourteenth century, but at any rate it would be cheaper to pursue him at Cheylesmore.

Presumably Agnes' claim was for between eight and ten pounds, as executor of her husband's will. But Robert de Everdon's executors, one of whom was Richard Belers, took their claim for a debt of eighteen pounds from John de Merynton to the Court of Common Pleas.[47] And Sir John Botiler of Exhall, who could no doubt afford it, decided to defend his case at Westminster rather than Cheylesmore. Believing that he had not had his just dues (in money or service) from his tenants, John and Alice Harnewode, Botiler seized their ox in distraint to compel them to pay up. The Harnewodes responded by suing Botiler and his servant Henry Baudy in the Cheylesmore court for illegally taking and detaining their beast. A lord of a manor was entitled to distrain for services due, so probably the Harnewodes intended to deny Botiler's right to them. If so, the case would be important to Botiler, who no doubt had other tenants who might try the same tactics. So he purchased a royal writ of *recordari*, which ordered the sheriff of Warwickshire to go with four knights to the Cheylesmore court, get a certified record of the proceedings so far, send it to Westminster, and notify the litigants to appear there.[48]

Probably a more typical case of debt than those involving the abbot of Coombe was the dispute in 1365 between Geoffrey atte Grene and the Stoke tiler, John Mariote. Mariote admitted owing twenty-eight pence, which he offered to pay, but Grene, through his attorney, claimed double the amount (a common penalty for failure to pay on time), plus two shillings damages. The court ruled in

Mariote's favour, and fined Grene for a false claim.[49] Mariote was a frequent litigant, perhaps because of the nature of his business (or the way he conducted it?). In August 1366, for instance, he was being sued because he had failed to produce on time five hundred tiles, which he had bargained to supply to Thomas de Merynton.[50]

The cases dealt with in the three-weeks court, should, if they had arisen within the city, have been brought before the portmanmoot, which, about 1355, was described as a court for small pleas, debts, and trespasses relating to leases and tenure.[51] With two courts operating within a quarter of a mile of each other, it is not surprising that there was sometimes confusion, or that Coventrians felt that, perhaps with a little legal manoeuvring, they had a choice of courts. Master William le Marshall sued Peter le Loche of Cotesbach in Leicestershire in the Cheylesmore court for breach of covenant and two counts of trespass. Marshall won the covenant case when Locke failed to do his law, but having started proceedings, apparently changed his mind about the other cases, and pleaded that as the trespasses had occurred within the city, jurisdiction belonged to the mayor and bailiffs. The court agreed, but of course fined Marshall for his invalid prosecution.[52] Possibly Marshall felt he would get a quicker judgment in the town court. Possibly he started a suit in both courts intending to abandon the least promising one. A century later, the corporation complained to the King that people who were not tenants of Cheylesmore manor were being encouraged by the steward to sue in its courts[53] (more cases meant more profit for the King's Cheylesmore estate, of course).

The routine regulation of communal agriculture was presumably a matter for the courts of the subordinate manors. But disputes between individuals which came before the three-weeks court illustrate Coventrians' involvement in the rural areas adjoining the city. Horses belonging to the quarry-owner Hugh le Webbe of Cook Street were alleged to have eaten Simon Hanvyle's corn at Stoke. This was only one of several pleas by Hanvyle and John Elys, against Webbe and William de Bitlesby. One other at least involved trespass in corn.[54] On the other side of the city, at Spon, Henry de Sutton's three cows got on to Richard le Bailiff's land, and ate grass worth forty pence. Richard impounded them, as he was entitled to do, but Henry broke down the barriers and rescued them, according to Richard, who claimed ten shillings damages. Henry denied all this, and undertook to do his law, but after some delay, he and Richard settled their dispute out of court.[55]

Other litigants' occupations link them to the city's industrial life. Thomas Baudy, wiredrawer, was sued for trespass by Sir Robert de Greseleye;[56] John de Hamslape, founder, sued Roger de Cumpton, mercer;[57] Richard de Oxenford, locksmith, was sued by Andrew de Napton.[58] Napton had property in Spon Street,[59] while Oxenford was located in Greyfriars Lane,[60] so one might have expected Napton to sue in the town court. But he must have had a holding outside the town in Spon as he owed suit from there to the view of frankpledge at Wolfpitlidyate,[61] so he took his case to the Cheylesmore court.

It is well known that the local courts, whose protracted proceedings were intended for those resident in their neighbourhood, or tenants of their lord, could not cater for travelling merchants who needed quick settlements of disputes before moving on, and so 'courts of piepowder'[62] grew up at fairs and markets, where cases involving itinerant traders might be concluded in a day, or at latest, by the end of a fair. A piepowder court operated in Coventry as part of the jurisdiction of the portmanmoot, but there is vestigial evidence of an occasional court of the same kind at Cheylesmore. Attached to the court rolls for 41 and 42 Edward III is a smaller piece of parchment belonging to the next year (a year for which the routine court rolls are lost).[63] The document is headed 'Pleas of the Spicers at Cheylesmore' (*Placita apud Cheillesmor de pipull*[64]), Friday after the Feast of the Assumption, 43 Edward III (17th August 1369). The day of the week itself suggests a special court, for the normal three-weekly courts at Cheylesmore were held on Saturdays. Only one item of business was recorded; John Swyneshed of Coventry, spicer *(pipull')* sued Henry Hurre of Hereford, spicer *(pipull')*, for breach of an agreement. Hurre's horse and a bundle *(fardellum)* ,presumably of merchandise, together worth sixty shillings, were attached to ensure his appearance in court. Afterwards *(postea)* (which could have been the same day), the disputants agreed, with the consent of the court. Swyneshed was a substantial citizen, described as a merchant in 1354, when he took a lease of four shops in Bayley Lane.[65] He was a guild member,[66] had been bailiff in

Illustration of the Coventry Watchtower and Stocks. From a sketch by Dr Nathaniel Troughton. PA1/3/39. *Reproduced courtesy of Coventry Archives.*

Illustration of a beggar with leg strapped up and man in stocks, 3rd quarter 15th Century. Detail from MS. Rawl D. 1220, fol, 25v. Astronomical treatise, English, 3rd quarter 15th century. *Reproduced courtesy of the Bodleian Library, University of Oxford.*

1363, and was to be mayor in 1379. Obviously the town's portmanmoot or the piepowder court would have been open to him for any dispute originating within their jurisdiction. The inference from the document must be that a fair where spicery was traded took place outside the town, perhaps in Cheylesmore Park, for which a special court was provided. On this occasion the court was not very profitable to the Black Prince, for the only income was the sixpence fine imposed on Henry Hurre.

Returning to the regular three-weekly court, it is clear that prosecutions for small debts took up much of its time. Allegations of detention of goods or animals which the plaintiffs claimed were theirs also occur from time to time, as do pleas of covenant, that is, failure to abide by a written agreement, and we have noted a single attempt to use the court to compel a reluctant servant to serve her agreed term.[67] But the great majority of cases were pleas of trespass, a wide-ranging term which could cover almost any wrong done by one man or woman to another, from letting animals stray into corn to assaults and behaviour approaching robbery with violence. The responsibilities of unsuccessful defendants, however, were limited to compensation and damages. Thus an abusive brawl at Styvechale led to an unrealistic claim for a hundred shillings damages from John le Pouchmaker, for assaulting John de Bury's wife Felise (Pouchemaker claimed she abused him and attacked him in his own house).[68] More serious, we would consider, was the case of John le Fytheler, whose trespass John le Walsh complained of in May 1365. Five courts later, the two confronted each other, when Walsh related that Fytheler had assaulted him at Spon and also killed his cocks and hens worth two shillings and carried them off, for which he claimed forty pence damages. Fytheler denied all this and was ordered to do his law at the next court.[69] The record is missing, but if Fytheler failed to clear himself he would only have to compensate Walsh in money; there would no penalty implying the community's disapproval of his violent proceedings.

But the actions of the Coventrian John de Cruddeworth and his servant John, which might appear to us to differ only in scale from Fytheler's attack on the hen-run and its owner, were treated more seriously as a breach of the king's peace, and thus the concern of the bi-annual court leet at Wolfpitlidyate. The two Johns broke into the premises of Henry le Wryghte (otherwise Henry atte Heth, wright) in Foleshill, and drove off two horses and a mare, valued at £3. The two 'tithingmen' for Foleshill, Walter Stritt and William le Carter, presented the offences at the court leet in April 1364, when Cruddeworth was fined elevenpence for taking the animals, and forty pence for the more serious offence of housebreaking, for which his servant was fined two shillings. But they were not prepared to let the matter rest there, and proceeded to sue the two tithing men in the three-weeks court for a false presentment to the court leet. In October the parties put themselves on a 'view', that is, the verdict of a jury, who found for the tithingmen and the two Johns were fined again.[70] No doubt there was more behind this incident than appears in the court roll, as Cruddeworth and Heth were suing each other for trespass a year later.[71]

It is common in the fourteenth century to find instances of men, often prominent citizens, apparently behaving like hooligans or brigands. Often reluctant to endure the law's delays, they took swift and direct means to secure what they claimed as their rights. But this could hardly be pleaded in defence of the two mercers William de Keresleye and John Chaloner, who, with John de Hamslape, founder, of Spon Street, the chaplain William de Lalleford, and one Henry, the second chaplain of Holy Trinity Church, were protagonists in the eternal battle between game preservers and poachers. They fished in the private waters of the Black Prince, broke the hedges of Cheylesmore Park, and poached the rabbits and deer which escaped onto their own land. Fines ranging from two to four shillings were imposed by the court leet.[72]

So far, none of those who accused these men of making off with their property charged them with the capital crime of theft. The ominous words 'feloniously stole' were not used. When they were, the charge was too serious to be tried at Wolfpitlidyate. For instance, in 1357, John Engleis was accused of taking Simon Hanvyld's mare at Biggin. It was worth thirteen shillings and fourpence, only a quarter of the value of the animals which Cruddeworth and his servant took from Wright, but 'the words of felony' appeared in the accusation. So Engleis was charged before the mayor and bailiffs of Coventry, who committed him to their prison to await trial before the king's justices of gaol delivery. After nearly a year in gaol, the jury found him not guilty: otherwise he could have been hanged.[73]

So far, it looks as if, outside the city, we have a neat system of courts appropriate to the degrees of delinquency. Civil actions, as we would call them, go to the three-weeks court. If breach of the peace is involved, the offenders are presented, and fined if guilty, at the court leet. Alleged felonies go before the mayor and bailiffs, in whose prison the accused await their trial before the itinerant judges.

In practice, things were not so tidy. By ancient custom, prosecution of felons could start in the court leet,[74] and in 1380, the leet jury presented two men from Sowe for feloniously stealing property worth ten shillings, and taking an ox at Wyken.[75] No doubt, like those charged before the mayor and bailiffs, they would await the visit of the king's justices. More important, the judicial functions of the ancient leet were being superceded by the powers entrusted to the recently established justices of the peace, who dealt widely with trespasses which involved breaches of the peace or violence, infringements of the labour laws, and trading offences, including regrating, buying goods or provisions to sell again in the same market (with the possibility of creating a monopoly). The first indictments for felonies could be made in their court, though trial was usually left to the itinerant judges. By 1377, the date of the first surviving records of the justices' sessions, the court leet can only have been making a marginal contribution to the fight against serious crime. Only the disputes and claims for damages in the courts baron (the three-weekly courts), were unaffected by the growth of the justices' powers.[76]

These powers rested on commissions from the king's chancery, appointing justices by name; they could be ended by revocation. The mayor and bailiffs' jurisdiction derived, of course, from the charter of June 1345, which also granted them a gaol where they could hold those from within the jurisdiction of the Cheylesmore view of frankpledge awaiting trial by the king's justices.[77] The court leet's pedigree was much longer. Like the three-weeks court, it had its origins in the liberty which the earls of Chester had of withdrawing their men and tenants from the hundred and county courts, and setting up their own courts, under their own stewards. Bi-annual meetings at Woltpitlidyate replaced the Sheriffs 'tourn', a six-monthly visit to the hundred to see that offences were recorded, and to check frankpledge, that is, that men were in their 'tithings' (groups responsible for their members' good behaviour, and for producing accused members in court). The Wolfpitlidyate leet was invariably designated 'view of frankpledge' in its rolls. Indictments for felony were received by the court as they had been by the sheriff.

By the fourteenth century the tithings, originally groups of ten families, had been replaced by the communities of the nineteen villages and hamlets mentioned in the Tripartite Indenture as being 'within the view of frank- pledge of Cheylesmore'. Sometimes two villages were linked, for example Radford and Keresley, but normally two tithingmen from each place attended at Wolfpitlidyate (with some defaults), and reported on their community. Sometimes they only reported 'all is well' (*omnia bene*), and the tithing-man for Asthill could only report that no-one lived there, presumably not even himself! At other times, they presented cases of housebreaking, assaults where blood had been drawn, and cases where the hue and cry had been raised, calling on people to pursue and arrest peace-breakers.[78]

In 1367 the Whitley tithingmen depicted a deplorable state of disorder. Perhaps it originated in a tavern brawl, as it included Robert Luttelman, the husband of an ale-wife, and two of his servants. Luttelman and Robert le Reve had drawn each other's blood, and each raised the hue and cry against his antagonist. Robert de Flore and John 'le Walkersman' likewise. John le Pouchemaker had drawn blood from the tithingman Ralph le Reve, who had been joined by Robert le Reve to raise hue and cry against John. Luttelman had raised it against Robert Page. Maud Miles had raised it against Luttelman's servant Thomas, who had drawn blood from her. Thomas' servant, another Maud, along with Alice de Brinklow, had justly raised it against William Malsun, who had unjustly raised it against them. Those considered guilty were fined twopence, threepence, or fourpence, except for Robert le Reve, whose assault on Luttelman cost him a shilling.[79] The Whitleyans were, of course, not the only brawlers, and hue and cry could be

Two drinking vessels of the 14th Century.
Discovered during archaeological investigation in Coventry.
Reproduced courtesy of the Herbert Art Gallery and Museum.

raised for other misdemeanours as well as common assaults. John of the Orchard, having taken goods or animals in distraint, Richard de Ferby's servant Peter 'rescued' them, whereupon John alerted the community by blowing a horn.[80]

The tithingmen were also the 'ale-tasters' for their villages, and presented brewers and tavern keepers for 'breaking the assize of ale'. Usually no details are vouchsafed, but in 1367 the Exhall tithingmen said that the two ale-wives there charged three half pence a gallon, and also sold by the 'dish' and 'cup', which were unauthorized measures.[81] It became customary in the course of time for a regular fine to be the equivalent of a licence to carry on brewing, but this practice had evidently not yet become general, for in 1380 two people were fined for omitting to send for the ale-taster. No doubt 'good ale needs no bush', but John Huwet's wife in Styvechale was fined an extra penny for selling hers without putting up a sign.[82] Besides the brewers there were the regraters' or tapsters, who bought ale to sell again - an offence - who were also fined. Most likely they were keepers of small taverns without the facilities for brewing or the customers to make it worthwhile. One, Margaet Whitele of Whitley, who sold a pot (olla) of ale, was so poor that she was let off her fine.[83]

As everyone drank ale, one can get a rough idea from the amount of brewing in a village, not so much of how many people lived there, but of how frequented it was. In 1373, no brewers were presented in Spon, but the regrater John atte Spon apparently provided for those not inclined to walk the short distance into Spon Street inside the city. Thirsts were slaked in Foleshill by a regrater, and three men who in six months made sixteen brews between them. In neighbouring Exhall there were the same number of brewers and brews, but no regrater. Drinkers in Whitley had to rely on Richard Lithulph's wife, who made ten brews, and Thomas Page's wife who was a regrater. In Wyken (with part of Sowe), the tithingman, William Repyndon, presented his own wife as a brewer along with William Sewall. Each had brewed three times, and was fined sixpence. But their output was trivial by comparison with the two men and a woman in Stoke who made forty-nine brews in the six months.[84]

Occasionally tithingmen reported roads needing repair. In 1364 a

Coventry ironmonger, Richard de Teynton, was blamed for the bad condition of Bushel Lane in Radford.[85] Watercourses also needed the court's oversight. People were presented for neglecting their obligations to scour specified ditches.[86] Sherlingsforth alias Serleford in Foleshill was blocked through the fault of Robert Ingram in 1373,[87] and in 1364 a stopped-up ditch was blamed on the Prior of Coventry, who was presented at the same court for a more serious matter, namely fencing off land in Keresley which should have been open as common pasture every third year.[88] The commoners' rights were also threatened by Henry le Shepherd of Spon, who was alleged to have no pasture rights but had six score 'alien' sheep grazing on commons to the west of the city.[89]

The lord of the manor's rights in the soil and what lay beneath were enforced by the court. John le Carter and William de Coppeston were fined in 1367 for digging clay in Stoke,[90] probably for the tilers, and John de Ryeton in 1380 for getting sand in Wyken.[91] Felling trees and cutting wood were also finable activities.[92] Straying animals, which went to the lord if not claimed, were duly noted and valued,[93] as was a 'stray' half yard of cloth, worth threepence, which turned up in Exhall.[94]

In April 1380, after Richard II had succeeded his father as lord of Cheylesmore, the Stoke tithingmen presented one of the Coventry bailiffs, Richard de Teynton, the ironmonger, for what seemed to be an attempt to extend the limits of the corporation's authority. He had gone beyond the bounds of the town to Stoke, and without a warrant, 'within the foreign of the lord king' arrested John and Thomas Mariot, taken them off to Coventry gaol, and only released them when they paid a fine of five shillings and sixpence.[95] The boundary between the city and Stoke was at Jabett's Ash (or Jabett's Pit), adjoining what is now Stoke Green. Beyond the city limits the corporation's powers are not always clear. Their gaol was to hold prisoners from anywhere within the Cheylesmore view of frankpledge. They could try the lesser offenders, and hold those charged with serious crimes pending trial by the itinerant judges,[96] as has been said. Whether they were entitled to go beyond their boundary to arrest minor offenders without a warrant, is not clear. Certainly the tithingmen's presentment indicates a vigilant attitude towards the corporation officials outside the city limits.

View of the Greyfriars Gate which was the entrance into the city on the West side, Greyfriars Tower and spire standing alone.

The Greyfriars settled in Coventry in about 1234. Little is known about the buildings of the house of the Franciscans or Greyfriars apart from its 14th century church, the central tower of which still survives. In the 14th century there was a gate in the park wall for the use of sick friars. The stone church, which survived until the Dissolution, was probably started c. 1359 when the friars received permission to take stone for their buildings from a quarry in Cheylesmore park; this grant was confirmed in 1378. The house was dissolved in 1542 and the buildings, apart from the church tower, were quickly demolished.

Reproduced courtesy of the Coventry Archives.

Conjectural Plan of Grey Friars Church by William Reader, 1829.
The size and shape of the church can be partly reconstructed from the
surviving work at the crossing, from a document quoted by W. G.
Fretton and thought to give the measurements of the building before its
demolition, and from excavations on the site in 1829. This plan
emphasised the size and importance of the chancel, used only by the
friars, and its separation from the more public parts of the church such
as the nave and aisles. *Reproduced courtesy of Coventry Archives.*

As well as the tithingmen, the leet jury made presentments. In 1379 they presented John Frenchman of Wyken as 'a common piker [petty thief] of sheaves and geese, against the assize',[97] and in 1373, Thomas le Cartwright for a 'rescue' on the bailiff and constable (that is, he had forcibly retrieved animals or goods which the officials were taking in distraint on the orders of the court).[98] The same jury presented the Greyfriars, whose house adjoined Cheylesmore manor house. The friars had benefited from the patronage of earl Ranulph Blundeville and his successors at Cheylesmore, but the jury declared that the hedge they had raised adjoining the hall at Cheylesmore constituted a nuisance to the Black Prince, and ordered them to demolish it under penalty of six shillings and eightpence.[99]

Who, besides the tithingmen, assembled at Wolfpitlidyate, perhaps to be placed on the jury, or in other ways contribute to the proceedings? As one would expect, the lords of the subordinate manors, including the Clerks and the Darkers from Coventry, owed suit at the court leet. Others from the city were the Freberns, doing suit for their holding in Whitley. Again, the lord of Tackleye in Oxfordshire, owed suit.[100] But fines in lieu of attendance were acceptable, and it was mostly humbler people who attended to conduct the business under the direction of the steward. Sufficient numbers were assured by linking the obligation to attend to the tenure of certain properties in the subordinate manors. When in 1370 the Coventry dyer, John de Corby and his wife Agnes acquired a messuage and land in Stoke on a hundred-year lease, they not only had to pay a token chief rent to the lords of Stoke, but also to attend at Wolfpitlidyate twice a year.[101] They were, of course, by no means the only Coventrians under that obligation. Lists of those who were fined for evading it include familiar Coventry names, especially in Spon.[102]

Our broken run of Cheylesmore court rolls ends in 1380, and a presentment for felony appears in the last roll of the court leet. Apart from an occasional fragment, there are no more rolls for over a century. When they resume, we see the leet almost entirely concerned with breaches of the assize of ale, taking of excessive toll by millers, unscoured ditches, and stray animals, though vestiges of its old jurisdiction appear occasionally as the tithingmen present brawlers for making an affray against the king's peace, and drawing blood, for which they are fined fourpence or eightpence.[103] There are no separate rolls for the three-weekly court baron, but it was still functioning in the fifteenth century. In 1434 the bailiff accounted for a year's income from seventeen courts (baron) and two leets,[104] and, as we have seen, thirty years later, the corporation complained of the steward's poaching of cases which should have been tried in the town courts.[105]

Originally the leet at Wolfpitlidyate was merely the 'foreign' half of the earls of Chester's court for their Coventry estate. The other half, the view of frankpledge within the town itself, was the main item of litigation between Queen Isabella and the Prior in 1336.[106] Its records are vestigial until the fifteenth century, by which time it is clearly the legislative body for the town, but no longer a court for trial of offences,[107] which were then dealt with either in the mayor and the bailiffs' court, or, increasingly, by the justices of the peace.

Glossary

Assize of Bread and Ale: the right of the lord of the manor to enforce the national regulations concerning the price and quality of the sale of loaves and beer. It usually accompanied the view of frankpledge (see below)

Attach: to arrest in order to secure the presence of the accused before the appropriate court, either by keeping him in prison, or by seizure of his goods and chattels, or by finding pledges (sureties, guarantors) for his appearance in court.

Charter of Incorporation: royal grant to an urban community recognizing its existence as a legal, self-governing entity, headed by a mayor and council with a common seal.

Clerk: man in holy orders; not permitted to marry if he attained the order of sub-deacon (or above - deacon, priest, bishop); if accused of a felony before a secular court a clerk could plead 'benefit of clergy', and, on proof of clerical status, then could only be tried in an ecclesiastical court, and punished according to church law.

Coffer: a strong box for keeping money or valuables in.

Collusive action: a legal action brought against a defendant with his agreement for the benefit of the plaintiff.

Corrody: free quarters and maintenance, often in a monastery.

Court baron: the court of a manor in which the lord exercises jurisdiction over his tenants by virtue of the land they hold from him. Would deal mainly with rents, services and rights of succession to holdings.

Court leet: the court of a manor in which the lord exercises powers of law enforcement originally possessed by the king, sometimes given to him by royal grant, sometimes usurped, often claimed by prescription for example, the view of frankpledge (see below): a sort of privatisation of royal justice.

Felony: any serious crime carrying the death penalty (or outlawry if the accused failed to appear in court) and confiscation of property. Serious crime began with grand larceny (see below) and extended to rape, murder, etc.

Gaol delivery: usually twice yearly itinerant royal justices (justices of assize) visited the public prisons and tried or acquitted the prisoners held there. Thus the gaols were 'delivered' of their inmates.

Indict: formally to accuse a person of an offence against the law before a court.

Larceny: theft; petty larceny if the value of the stolen goods was 12d or less; grand larceny if more.

Liberty(ies): the right(s) of a lord or corporation to exercise certain jurisdictional powers in a given area, a manor or city for example, delegated by the king. Sometimes called a franchise.

Mainour: a stolen good found in a thief's possession on his arrest.

Mainpernor: a surety or pledge for an accused person's appearance in court on a specified day (modern equivalent is the person who puts up bail).

Mash-fat (massefat): a vat or vessel used in brewing to mix malt with warm water to form wort.

Merchant guild: an association of the leading merchants of a city or town which often evolved into the urban community's governing body.

Messuage: a plot of land with a dwelling upon it, usually substantial in size (more than a mere cottage).

Plead clergy: to claim benefit of clergy (see Clerk above).

Pleas of the crown: crimes (felonies or trespasses against the king's peace) reserved to the king. The fines or forfeitures imposed on the convicted criminals also belong to the king. He could in particular instances grant these to another body as a special favour.

Portmoot or Portmanmote: the borough court, presided over by the mayor or bailiffs, the key institution in an urban community's control of its own affairs, as, for example, in Coventry.

Suit of court: the obligation of the tenants of a lord to attend his court.

Surety: see mainpernor (above).

Tithing man: the head (or chief pledge) of a tithing, generally a group of ten or twelve men in a village or township responsible for each other's law-abiding behaviour under the frankpledge system (see below). However, there were variations. In the hamlets which were part of the manor of Coventry or Cheylesmore, a tithing man or two represented the whole settlement and reported wrongdoings of its inhabitants to the court leet at Wolfpitlidyate.

Trailbaston: the offence of assaulting a person with a cudgel, club or staff with a view to robbery (original meaning: carrying a club).

Trespass: a criminal action short of felony against a man or woman's person, landed property or possessions, e.g. assault, shedding blood, housebreaking etc., causing a breach of the king's peace.

View of frankpledge: a system of maintaining law and order in the absence of a police force. With some exceptions and regional variations, every man over 12 was to be in a tithing (see above). They were responsible for each other's good behaviour by presenting any member of the group who committed an offence to the appropriate court for trial, or face paying a collective fine if they failed to do so. Twice yearly the sheriff checked that every man was in a tithing at a special session of the hundred court attended by the tithing-men (see above). This became known as the sheriff's 'turn' and the 'view of frankpledge'. Some lords and some municipal authorities acquired the right to hold the view of their tenants in their own courts, and to deal with the offences which the tithing-men presented (see Court leet above).

Vouch: (usually with to warrant or to warranty) to summon a person into court to guarantee the truth of a statement.

Sources - with abbreviated references

Manuscript Sources

Public Record Office (P.R.O.)
Register of St. Mary's Cathedral Priory. E164/21.
Court of Common Pleas. CP40/311; 40/174; 40/3/3.
Pipe Roll 24 Edw. III. E372/195.
Inquistiones ad quod damnum. E143/195; 201.
Court Rolls of the Manor of Cheylesmore &Wolfpitlydiate, Court
Baron and View of Frankpledge. SC2/207/17-20, 22, 23.
Court of the King's Bench. KB27/259.
Rolls of the Justices of the Peace (Coventry). E101/121.
Coventry Coroner's Rolls. JUST2/180; 182; 189; 191.
Rolls of the Justices of Labourers. JUST1/971; 3/146.
Rolls of Goal Delivery. JUST3/140; 159; 160; 167; 173; 177.
Contributions of Coventrians to the levy of 1322. E179/242/94.

Warwickshire County Record Office (W.R.O.)
Deeds of Holy Trinity Church, Coventry. DR429/10A

Coventry City Archives (C.C.A.)
Corporation Deeds and Drapers' Company Deeds -
Fourteenth Century.

Birmingham Reference Library (B.R.L.)
Historical Records of the City of Coventry I - Select Records Local
History Collection - no.297838-40. (H.R.C.C.)

Shakespeare Birthplace Trust Record Office, Stratford-upon-Avon. (S.B.T.)
Gregory Hood Deeds - Typescript Calendars. DR10/284.
Coventry Hundred Rolls. DR18/31/3.

Lincolnshire Archives
Jarvis. I/13/3/2.

University of London Library

The Fuller Collection (typescript), ed. D.E. Greenway, 1980, includes documents relating to Coventry, II, 16, 10.

Printed Sources

Public Record Office (P.R.O.)
Calendars of Charter Rolls. (C.Ch.R.)
Calendars of Close Rolls. (C.C.R.)
Calendars of Patent Rolls. (C.P.R.)
Catalogue of Ancient Deeds, III, IV, V. (C.A.D.)
Calendars of Inquisitions Post Mortem, VII. (C.I.P.M.)
Calendars of Fine Rolls. (C.F.R.)
Register of Edward the Black Prince.
Treaty Rolls, i) 1235-1325, ii) 1337-1339.

Dugdale Society Publications

VI Lay Subsidy Rolls for Warwickshire, 6 Edw.III, 1332, ed. W.F.Carter, 1926.
XI, XV, XVIII *Warwickshire Feet of Fines*
      Vol. I 1195 - 1284, ed. F.C. Wellstood, 1932.
      Vol. II 1284 - 1345, ed. F.T.S. Goughton, 1939.
      Vol. III 1345 - 1509, ed. W.Cooper, 1943.
XIII *Register of the Guild of Holy Trinity,* ed. M.D. Harris, 1935.
XVI *Rolls of Warwickshire and Coventry Sessions of the Peace,* 1377-1397, ed. E.G.Kimball, 1939. *(R.W.C.S.P.)*
XVII *The Statute Merchant Roll of Coventry*, 1392 - 1416, ed. A. Bearwood, 1939.
XXXII *The Langley Cartulary,* ed. P.R.Coss, 1980.

Selden Society Publications

23 *Select Cases concerning the Law Merchant,* ed. C. Gross, 1908.
55 *Select Cases in the Court of the King's Bench under Edward I*, ed. G.O.Sayles, 1936.
61 *Year Books of Edward II*, 11 Edw.II 1317-18, ed. J.P. Collas and W.Holdsworth, 1942.
97 *The Eyre of Northamptonshire* Vol. 1, ed. D.W. Sutherland, 1938

Miscellaneous

Coss, P.R., *The Early Records of Medieval Coventry*, British Academy Records of Social and Economic History, New Series XI, Oxford, 1986.

Harris, M.D., *The Coventry Leet Book or Mayor's Register,* Early English Text Society, Original Series, 134-5, 138, 146, London 1907-13.

Jeaffreson, J.C., *A Calendar of Rolls in the Muniment Room of St. Mary's Hall,* Coventry 1896.

Lunt, W.E. and Graves, E.B., *Accounts rendered by the Papal Collection in England,* 1317 - 18, Philadelphia, 1986.

Pelham, R.A., The Early Wool Trade in Warwickshire and the Rise of the Merchant Middle Class, *Transactions of the Birmingham Archaeological Society* (T.B.A.S.) LXIII.

Pike, L.O., *Year Books of Edward III*, 16 Edward III, 1342 - 3, Rolls Series, (R.S.).

Putnam, B.H., *The Enforcement of the Statute of Labourers during the first decade after the Black Death,* 1349 - 59, New York 1908.

Richardson, H.G. and Sayles, G.O., *Rotuli Parliamentorum Hactenus Inediti,* Camden Society, 3rd Series, 51, 1935.

Sharp, T., *Illustrative papers on the History and Antiquities of the City of Coventry*, (ed. W.G.Fretton), Birmingham 1871.

Lay Subsidy Roll for Warwickshire of 1327, Transactions of the Midland Record Society, Supplement to Vol.5, 1901.

Notes

Introduction:
The Local Jurisdictions in Coventry

1. P.R.O. JUST3/142m.15; H.R.C.C. I, f.175
2. P.R.O. JUST3/140m.3; H.R.C.C. I, f.172

Chapter 1: The Coroner in Action

1. P.R.O. JUST2/180, 182 passim. The coroners' rolls on which the following account is based are not original records made at the inquests, but compilations, written up from the contents of the coroners' files for submission to the Justices of the Kings Bench when they came to Coventry in 1387 and 1397 (Table by R.F. Hunnisett in *American Journal of Legal History*, III (1959) 212-213, 344-346). Thus John de Baldeswell's roll, the first we have, was written about thirty years after the events it records. Only the rolls submitted in 1387 give dates both for the inquests and the finding of the bodies, and it could be that the former were added by the compiler to give an impression of efficiency. On the other hand the Coventry coroners' district was small and compact and there is no obvious reason why they should not have held their inquests promptly.

Discussing 'The Reliability of Historical Evidence' (in D.A. Bullough and R.L. Storey (Ed.) *The Study of Medieval Records* (Oxford, 1971), Mr. Hunnisett has shown that we cannot take the coroners' rolls to be accurate in every detail, and we ourselves doubt for instance, whether William de Bury would remember in October the exact date when he stole a horse in March. Moreover, through some confusion, several inquests taken by John de Baldeswell appear twice on the roll and the entries are not always identical: John Brown, said in one version to have been found dead in Keresleye, where the inquest was held, is recorded as found in Coventry in the other entry; the fugitive killer William Nedler is said in one version to possess only a tapetum and two lintheamina worth altogether twelve pence; in the other he has unspecified chattels worth ten shillings (P.R.O. JUST2/180, mm. 1, 2). Mr Hunnisett, however, did not find that the broad outlines of juries' verdicts were untrustworthy, and we see no reason to doubt the main facts of deaths or crimes as recorded on the rolls.

2.W. Stubbs (Ed.), revised H.W.C. Davis, *Select Charters and other Illustrations of English Constitutional History* (Oxford, 1929), 254. For a full description of the work of the coroners see R.F. Hunnisett, *The Medieval Coroner* (Cambridge, 1961). General remarks about the coroner's powers and duties in the following pages owe much to Mr. Hunnisett's book.

3.*C.Ch.R.* II, 70.

4.G. Cross, *The Gild Merchant* (Oxford, 1890) II, 364-5; *C.P.R. 1266-72*, 278-9.

5.E.g. P. Coss, *The Early Records of Medieval Coventry* (1986) nos 38.2, 39.7, 52-54, 56-57 et seq. passim.

6.B.R.L. Ms 377487.

7.*C.Ch.R.* V, 48.

8.E.g. C.C.A. BA/B/A/68/2,   BA/B/P/431/5, BA/H/H/155/1, BA/B/P/433/20,   BA/B/K/1/1, BA/B/P/81/2,   BA/B/P/439/7, BA/H/H/160/1, BA/B/P/433/15,   BA/B/C/1/1,   BA/B/P/44/13, BA/B/A/50/4,   BA/B/P/163/5,   BA/H/H/301/12, BA/B/P/360/1, BA/H/H/108/5,   BA/B/A/78/23, BA/H/H/278/24,   BA/B/A/78/25-26, BA/H/H/436/1,   BA/B/A/44/12,   BA/B/P/435/3; *C.A.D.* II, B3722.

9.R.H.C. Davis, *Early History of Coventry,* Dugdale Society Occasional Paper No.24 (Oxford 1976), 26-27.

10.Coss, *Early Records*, passim; P.R.O. E164/21, ff. 96v-112v; C.C.A. Borough Archive (BA) deeds temp. Edward II, 1-8 Edwards III passim.

11.Coss, *Early Records*, nos 38.2, 39.7, 39.10.

12.P.R.O. JUST2/180, 182, 189, 191. These rolls cover approximately one third of the period 1354-97.

13.There are extensive extracts from these rolls in the Historical Records of the City of Coventry, Vol. 1 (H.R.C.C.), B.R.L. Ms. 297838.

14.*C.Ch.R.* V, 243; P.R.O. E368/143, Communia, Hilary rot V.

15.P.R.O. JUST2/180, 182, 189, 191.

16.P.R.O. JUST2/191 m.3.

17.Hunnisett, *Medieval Coroner*, 21.

18.Keresley and Caludon, P.R.O. JUST2/180 m.2; 189 m.2; H.R.C.C. I, 235, 241.

19.P.R.O. JUST2/182 m.1.

20.P.R.O. JUST2/191 m.3.

21.P.R.O. JUST2/191 m.2.

22.P.R.O. JUST2/180 m.1.

23.P.R.O. JUST2/180 m.3.

24.P.R.O. JUST2/191 m.4; H.R.C.C. I, 251v-252.

25.P.R.O. JUST2/189 mm. 2 and 3; H.R.C.C. I, 241v, 245v.

26.P.R.O. JUST2/180 m.3 dorse.

27.P.R.O. JUST2/189 m.2.

28.P.R.O. JUST2/189 m.3; H.R.C.C. I, 245v, 246v.

29.Hunnisett, *Medieval Coroner*, 2-3.

30.Hunnisett, *Medieval Coroner*, 30-31.

31.*C.C.R.* 1333-37, 410-11.

32.*C.Ch.R.* V, 33-34, 39-40, 47-48; *C.P.R. 1345-48*, 20-21; B.R.L. Ms. 377478; C.C.A. BA/G/A/3/4.

33.P.R.O. JUST2/180, 182, 189, 191 passim.

34.P.R.O. JUST2/180 m.1; JUST 1/971 rot.1, dorse; *Feet of Fines for Warks* III no. 2217.

35.P.R.O. JUST2/180 m.1; 182 m.2.

36.Hunnisett, *Medieval Coroner*, 30, 122.

37.P.R.O. JUST2/182.

38.P.R.O. JUST2/191 m.2 dorse.

39.P.R.O. JUST2/180 m.3 dorse.

40.P.R.O. JUST2/189 m.2; H.R.C.C. I, 241v.

41.P.R.O. JUST2/180 m.1.

42.P.R.O. JUST2/191 m.6 dorse; H.R.C.C. I, 254v-255.

43.P.R.O. JUST2/189 m.2; H.R.C.C. I, 241v-242.

44.P.R.O. JUST2/191 m.7; H.R.C.C. I, 255v-256. The second John is called son (filius) of the parson in the verdict, but 'Personservant' in the writ calling for the indictment to be sent to the Chancery.

45.P.R.O. JUST2/180, 182, 189, 191, passim.

46.P.R.O. JUST2/180, 182, 189, 191, passim.

47.P.R.O. JUST2/191 m.6 dorse; H.R.C.C. I, 255; *C.P.R. 1391-96*, 334.

48.P.R.O. JUST2/180 m.4; JUST2/191 m.2 dorse; JUST2/189 m.2 dorse; for Katherine Scarlet (H.R.C.C. I, 242v).

49. P.R.O. JUST2/182 m.1 dorse; JUST2/189 mm. 2 dorse, 3; H.R.C.C. 1, 243v, 246-246v.

50. P.R.O. JUST2/189 m.2; H.R.C.C. I, 240v.

51. P.R.O. JUST2/189 m.3; H.R.C.C. I, 245-245v.

52. P.R.O. JUST2/180 m.4; JUST2/191 m.2.

53. P.R.O. JUST2/182 m.1, dorse; JUST2/191 m.6; H.R.C.C. I, 253v.

54. E.g. Hunnisett, *Medieval Coroner*, 35.

55. P.R.O. JUST2/182 m.1 dorse.

56. P.R.O. JUST2/189 m.2; H.R.C.C. I, 242-242v.

57. P.R.O. JUST2/180 m.1.

58. P.R.O. JUST2/182 m.1.

59. P.R.O. JUST2/182 m.2.

60. P.R.O. JUST2/189 m.2 dorse; H.R.C.C. I, 244.

61. P.R.O. JUST2/189 m.3 dorse; H.R.C.C. I, 247.

62. P.R.O. JUST2/180 m.1; JUST2/191 m.3.

63. P.R.O. JUST2/182 m.2; JUST2/189 mm. 2, 3; H.R.C.C. I, 240, 247v.

64. P.R.O. JUST2/180 m.4.

65. P.R.O. JUST2/191 m.6; H.R.C.C. I, 254-254v.

66. P.R.O. JUST2/191 m.8 dorse; H.R.C.C. I, 257-257v.

67. P.R.O. JUST2/180 m.1 dorse.

68. P.R.O. JUST2/180 mm.1, 2 dorse.

69. P.R.O. JUST2/189 m.2 dorse; H.R.C.C. I, 242v-243.

70. P.R.O. JUST2/189 m.2; H.R.C.C. I, 240v.

71. P.R.O. JUST2/191 m.3.

72. P.R.O. JUST2/180 m.1; JUST2/189 m.2 dorse; JUST2/191 mm.3 dorse, 8 dorse; H.R.C.C. I, 257v.

73. Hunnisett, *Medieval Coroner*, 34-35; P.R.O. JUST2/189 mm.2, 3; JUST2/191 m.2.

74. Hunnisett, *Medieval Coroner*, 33-34; P.R.O. JUST2/191 m.3; JUST2/189 m.3; H.R.C.C. I, 247v; JUST2/189 m.2; H.R.C.C. I, 240.

75. *C.Ch.R.* V, 33-34, 39-40, 47-48; C.P.R. 1345-48, 20-21.

76. Hunnisett, *Medieval Coroner*, 113-4.

77. P.R.O. JUST2/180 mm.1, 4; JUST2/182 mm.1, 2; JUST2/189 mm.2, 2 dorse, 3, 3 dorse; JUST2/191 mm.2, 3, 3 dorse; H.R.C.C. I, 240-240v, 242v, 243, 244, 245, 247, 247v, 257v.

78. P.R.O. JUST2/189 mm.2, 2 dorse; JUST2/191 m.3; H.R.C.C. I, 240v, 243, 243v.

79. P.R.O. JUST2/191 m.2 dorse.

80. P.R.O. JUST2/180 mm.3 dorse, 4; JUST2/182 m.2.

81. P.R.O. JUST2/180 m.3 dorse.

82. P.R.O. JUST2/180 m.3 dorse.

83. P.R.O. JUST2/191 mm.2, 3 dorse, 4, 5, 6.

84. P.R.O. JUST2/191 m.3 dorse.

85. P.R.O. JUST2/191 m.6; H.R.C.C. I, 254.

86.P.R.O. JUST2/191 m.5; H.R.C.C. I, 252v.

87.P.R.O. JUST2/180 m.1 dorse (Coroner's Roll) and JUST3/140 m.3 dorse (Gaol Delivery Roll). There are discrepancies and probably errors in the dates given in the rolls for Bury's thefts at Newmarket and Coventry. Both give the date of Bury's first confession in Coventry gaol as Saturday after St. Simon and St. Jude, i.e. October 29th. But the coroner's roll says the Coventry thefts were on Friday after SS. Simon and Jude, which was November 4th. The gaol delivery roll gives Friday before the Saints' day, i.e. October 21st, which makes sense. But both rolls put the Newmarket theft on the Saints' day (October 28th), which would mean that Bury had travelled over 90 miles, been arrested, gaoled, and visited by the coroner in the space of 24 hours.

88.P.R.O. JUST2/140 m.3 dorse.

89.P.R.O. JUST2/146 m.4.

90.E.g. P.R.O. JUST2/191 m.5 dorse; H.R.C.C. I, 253v.

91.P.R.O. JUST2/180 m.3 dorse; H.R.C.C. I, 233v.

92.P.R.O. JUST2/191 m.5; H.R.C.C. I, 252-252v.

93.The roll of Thomas de Nassyngton, the Coventry coroner at the time, is missing, but Gogh's confessions are given on the gaol delivery roll (P.R.O. JUST3/167 m.95; H.R.C.C. I, 183-183v, 185v-186).

94.P.R.O. JUST2/167 m.71.

95.P.R.O. JUST2/180 m.1 dorse.

96.Hunnisett, *Medieval Coroner*, 47-48.

97.P.R.O. JUST2/180 m.3 dorse; JUST2/191 mm.9, 3.

98.P.R.O. JUST2/191 mm. 5- 5 dorse.

99.P.R.O. JUST2/191 m.2.

100.P.R.O. JUST2/191 mm.2,3.

101.Hunnisett, *Medieval Coroner*, 44-45.

102.P.R.O. JUST2/191 mm.2, 3.

103.P.R.O. JUST2/191 mm.2, 3.

104.P.R.O. JUST2/188 m.3; *R.W.C.S.P.*, 136, 175.

105.Hunnisett, *Medieval Coroner*, 48-50.

106.P.R.O. JUST2/180, 182, 189, 191. For a detailed list see Hunnisett in *American Journal of Legal History* Vol.3, 344-6.

107.P.R.O. JUST2/180 m.1 dorse.

108.*R.W.C.S.P.*, passim.

109.*R.W.C.S.P.*, 5-6.

110.*R.W.C.S.P.*, passim.

Chapter 2: The Prior's Coroner

1.Hunnisett, *Medieval Coroner*, 150, 162.

2.A. and E. Gooder, 'Coventry before 1355' in *Midland History*, VI, (1981), 9-10, 17; Coss, *Early Records*, xxix, and passim; P.R.O. E164/21 ff. 89-108; C.C.A. Borough Archive (BA) deeds, temp. Edw.II, 1-10, Edw.III passim.

3. See above p3.

4.C.C.A. PA468/11/244; C.C.A. BA/B/A/68/2, BA/B/P/433/20, BA/B/K/1/1, BA/B/P/81/2, BA/B/P/433/15, BA/H/H/404/1-2, BA/B/P/435/2,5, BA/B/P/44/13, BA/B/A/50/4, BA/H/H/301/12, BA/H/H/108/5, BA/B/A/78/23, BA/B/A/78/25-26, BA/H/H/436/1, BA/B/P/435/3; *C.A.D.*,II, B3722.

5.Davis, *Early History of Coventry*, 26, 27.

6.Hunnisett, *Medieval Coroner*, 116.

7.See below p19-25.

8.Coss, *Early Records*, xxix; C.C.A. BA/B/P/175/15.

9.Coss, *Early Records*, xxix and no. 258.

10.C.C.A. BA/B/A/29/3.

11. C.C.A. BA/B/A/29/3. William le Wode appears as coroner in the Priory Register (P.R.O. E164/21, f.98v) on a deed of 4th December 1313. But as the entries in the Register are copies and no more references to Wode have been found, this is probably a copyist's error.

12. C.C.A. BA/B/A/68/1. The replacement of all existing coroners was ordered on 15th January 1341 (Hunnisett, *Medieval Coroner*, 166; *C.C.R. 1339-41*, 607).

13.C.C.A. BA/H/H/48/19.

14.C.C.A. BA/B/P/266/8, BA/H/H/365/1, BA/B/A/82/2.

15.C.C.A. BA/H/H/50/4.

16.C.C.A. BA/B/A/80/2.

17.C.C.A. BA/H/H/48/20.

18.C.C.A. BA/B/P/402/2.

19.C.C.A. BA/B/P/433/13.

20.C.C.A. BA/B/P/435/3.

21.*Feet of Fines for Warks.*, II, ed. F.T.S. Goughton, Dugdale Society XV (1939), no. 1318; *C.A.D.*, III, A4277, IV, A7656; C.C.A. BA/H/H/407/2, BA/H/H/299/1.

22.*Feet of Fines for Warks.*, II, no. 1338; *C.P.R. 1321-24*, 172.

23.P.R.O. E179/242/94.

24.Transactions of the Midland Record Society V, Supplement (1901), 7-8; *The Lay Subsidy Roll for Warwickshire, 1332*, ed. W. F. Carter g Dugdale Society VI (1926), 44-45.

25.*Feet of Fines for Warks.*, II, no.1338; P.R.O. E326/6254.

26. C.C.A. BA/B/A/87/5.

27.*C.A.D.*, II, A4433.

28.*C.A.D.*, III, A6058.

29.*The Lay Subsidy Roll for Warwickshire, 6 Edw.III,1332*, 98/S/S

30.P.R.O. E164/21, ff. 107v-108, 109v; C.C.A. BA/B/P/414/1-2, BA/B/P/60/7, BA/B/A/12/8, BA/B/P/451/2-3, BA/H/H/72/1, BA/H/H/278/11, BA/H/H/384/1, BA/B/A/107/6, BA/B/P/15/1, BA/B/A/70/3, 5, BA/B/P/179/16, BA/H/H/48/18, BA/G/F/41/1,

BA/B/A/107/9, BA/B/P/451/9, BA deeds 13-16 Edw. III passim; C.C.A. PA468/11/116.

31.W.R.O., Holy Trinity Church Deeds DR429/18, 19 (Typescript calendar in C.C.A.).

32.*Feet of Fines for Warks*. II, 1788; P.R.O. CP40/310, attorney's roll ij dorse, vij; CP 40/311 rot. 193 dorse; CP 40/312 rot. 38 dorse, 135 dorse.

33.C.C.A. BA/B/P/80/4.

34.C.C.A. BA/F/A/23/1 f.88.

35.C.C.A. BA/H/H/260/1, BA/H/H/299/1, BA/H/H/301/9, BA/H/H/50/4, BA/H/H/301/4, BA/B /P/439/6, BA/H/H/278/16, BA/B/P/433/12, BA/B/P/352/7, BA/B/P/439/5, BA/B/P/433/3, BA/B/P/326/5, BA/H/H/164/5, BA/H/H/146/1, BA/B/P/352/8, BA/B/P/350/10, BA/H/H/173/3, BA/B/P/433/4, BA/B/P/357/1, BA/B/P/61/7, BA/B/A/54/12, BA/B/A/107/10, BA/B/P/431/4, BA/B/P/356/2, BA/H/H/301/14, BA/H/H/18/7, BA/B/P/433/17, BA/B/P/414/4, BA/H/H/48/20, BA/B/P/409/5.

36.P.R.O. C81/301/16533; *C.P.R. 1343-45*, 426, 490.

37.*C.P.R. 1343-45, 573*; *C.C.R. 1343-46*, 644.

38.C.C.A. BA/B/P/260/1.

39.*Feet of Fines for Warks*. III, 2032. This Simon, as a minor, was a ward of Edward II, but he was of age by 1332, probably by 1327, and died about 1376. He became a justice of labourers, and of the peace in Leicestershire, M.P. for the county, and steward of the honour of Leicester for John of Gaunt. Two inventories he made of documents kept at Gaunt's palace of the Savoy are still extant (*C.C.R. 1330-33*, 436; *C.C.R. 1343-46* to *1374-77* passim; *C.P.R. 1340-1377* passim; *Victoria County History, Leicestershire*, II, 97, note 12; R.H.C. Davis, *Medieval Cartularies of Great Britain* (1958), 148, quoting P.R.O. DL41/1/27 and 33). It is possible that it was this Simon and not the Coventry one who was commissioned to inquire about the attacks on William Walshman and the death of the abbot of Coombe.

40. *Transactions of the Midland Record Society* V, Supplement, 8.

41. Coss, *Early Records*, nos. 390, 393, 487, 488.

42. *C.F.R., 1319-27*, 104. List is P.R.O. E179/242/94.

43. Coss, *Early Records*, p.379.

44. M/S/McKisack, *The Fourteenth Century* (1959), 169; Hunnisett, *Medieval Coroner*, 166; C.C.A. Borough Archives deeds for the period 3 Edw.II to 14 Edw. III passim; P.R.O. E164/21 ff. 98v-108.

45. C.C.A. BA/H/H/214/1-2; Coss, *Early Records*, no.493; P.R.O. E164/21 f. 135v.

46. P.R.O. E164/21 ff. 114v-117; C.C.A. BA/B/A/107/12, BA/B/A/50/4, BA/H/H/108/6, BA/B/A/50/5; *C.P.R. 1350-54*, 443; *C.P.R. 1354-58*, 44; *C.P.R. 1358-61*, 36.

47. *C.P.R. 1324-27*, 127.

48. Coss, *Early Records*, nos. 390, 488, 493, 518.

49. Coss, *Early Records*, nos.39.1, 39.9.

50. Coss, *Early Records*, nos.138, 142, 215, 231, 233, 311, 364.

51. Coss, *Early Records*, no. 26.

52. Coss, *Early Records*, no. 138.

53. Coss, *Early Records*, xxix and passim; *C.A.D.* III, A4277; Holy Trinity Church deed W.R.O. DR429/10a; Gregory Hood deed S.B.T. DR10/324.

54. Coss, *Early Records*, nos. 625, 645; Gregory Hood deed S.B.T. DR10/325.

55. Coss, *Early Records*, nos. 367-369, 374.

56. C.C.A. BA/B/P/402/2, BA/B/P/400/4.

57. *C.A.D.* IV, A6608; P.R.O. E40/14840.

58. Coss, *Early Records*, no. 709.

59. Transactions of the Midland Record Society V, Supplement, 7; *Lay Subsidy Warks, 1332*, 46.

60. C.C.A. BA/A/D/7/1.

61. C.C.A. BA/B/P/400/2-3, BA/B/P/222/5, BA/H/H/404/1-2, BA/B/P/45/7.

62. C.C.A. BA/H/H/27/3; *Feet of Fines for Warks.*, II, 1822.

63. P.R.O. E164/21 f.109v.

64. Clerks who were not beneficed usually seem to have paid.

65. C.C.A. BA/B/P/138/4, BA/B/P/292/13-14, BA/B/A/54/11, BA/B/A/74/6.

66. *C.A.D.* IV, A6628; C.C.A. BA/B/P/400/4.

67. C.C.A. BA/B/P/433/3, BA/B/P/297/3.

68. C.C.A. BA/B/P/92/1; M.D. Harris, *The Coventry Leet Book or Mayor's Register*, Early English Text Society, 134 (1907), 449.

69. *Year Book of Edward III* (Rolls Series) VIII (year 16 pt. ii), 87-90.

70. C.C.A. BA/H/H/404/2, BA/B/P/92/1.

71. P.R.O. E164/21 f.109v; E42/233; C.C.A. BA/B/P/328/3, BA/B/A/11/1, BA/H/H/167/4.

72. C.C.A. BA/H/H/48/20, BA/B/A/78/21, BA/B/P/402/2, BA/B/P/400/4.

73. *C.A.D.* IV, A6608; C.C.A. BA/B/P/292/33.

74. Coss, Early Records, xxvi, xix, and passim where the surname is rendered as 'Baker'; C.C.A. BA/B/P/403/1, BA/B/P/138/4, BA/B/P/175/15.

75.C.C.A. BA/H/H/54/3, BA/H/H/34/2, BA/B/P/111/15-16, BA/B/P/246/2, BA/B/P/111/19, BA/B/P/433/10-11.

76.C.C.A. Borough Archive deeds of 15 Edw.III passim; BA/H/H/215/1, BA/B/P/266/8, BA/H/H/365/1, BA/B/A/82/2.

77.C.C.A. BA/B/P/403/1; *Feet of Fines for Warks.*, II, 174; P.R.O. CP40/310 rot.263.

78.*C.A.D.* III, A4332; C.C.A. BA/B/P/138/4, BA/B/P/355/2, BA/B/P/295/15.

79.P.R.O. E164/21 f.133v.

80.C.C.A. BA/B/P/324/1.

81.C.C.A. BA/H/H/224/2.

82.P.R.Coss (Ed.), *The Langley Cartulary*, Dugdale Society XXXII (1980), no. 322; P.R.O. CP40/210 rot.263.

83.S.B.T. DR10/332, 344, 346; *Feet of Fines for Warks.*, II, 1840, 1872.

84.S.B.T. DR10/344; C.C.A. BA/H/H/365/1.

85.C.C.A. BA/B/Q/16/1; *C.P.R. 1343-45*, 40 (this was not the chief rent which Baxtere acquired in 1340). The deed conveying the rent is endorsed 'Corpus Christi Hall' (de Aula Corporis Christi) and the rent is given as coming from the Hall in the great Trinity Guild deed of 20th September 1393 (BA/B/P/14/5). Henry and Agnes Baxtere appear in Mary Dormer Harris (ed.) *The Register of the Guild of the Holy Trinity*, Dugdale Society XIII, (1935), 10, immediately after Henry Mollyng a Master of St. John the Baptist's Guild.

86.P.R.O. CP40/310 rot.200.

87.C.C.A. PA468/D11/244; *C.A.D.* II, B3722; C.C.A. BA/H/H/139/1, BA/B/P/433/13-14, BA/B/A/68/2, BA/B/P/433/20, BA/B/K/1/1, BA/B/P/81/2, BA/B/P/433/15, BA/H/H/404/1-2, BA/B/P/435/2, 5, BA/B/P/44/13, BA/B/A/50/4, BA/H/H/301/12, BA/B/P/414/6,

BA/H/H/108/5, BA/B/A/78/23, 25, 26, BA/H/H/436/1, BA/B/P/435/3.

88.C.C.A. BA/B/A/83/1; P.R.O. E164/21 f.117v.

89.P.R.O. E164/21 f.119.

90.C.C.A. BA/B/P/434/4, BA/B/P/433/20.

Chapter 3: The Corporation's Coroner.

1.E.g. P.R.O. JUST3/140 mm.1, 2, 3, 3 dorse.

2.P.R.O. JUST3/159 m.10; JUST3/160 m.6; JUST3/167 m.22 dorse.

3.*C.Ch.R.* V, 243.

4.*C.Ch.R.* II, 70.

5.Hunnisett, *Medieval Coroner*, 150, 162.

6.P.R.O. C53/133 m.8.

7.See list p32; *Victoria County History, Warwickshire*, VIII, 157.

8.In 1406-7 - 'List of Mayors', *Coventry Municipal Handbook*.

9.Arthingworth, Waller and John de Baldeswell. *C.P.R. 1345-48*, 32.

10.C.C.A. BA/B/P/295/3.

11.C.C.A. BA/B/P/201/2 dorse, BA/B/P/359/28.

12.C.C.A. BA/A/C/8/4.

13.Bruggeford, Thos. de Baldeswell, Ocham, Nassyngton, Attleborough, Baron. See the list of coroners on page 32-33.

14.*R.W.C.S.P.*, 73, 74, 78, 80, 83.

15.Hunnisett, *Medieval Coroner*, 120-1.

16.P.R.O. JUST2/180, 182 passim. These were the rolls prepared for the visit of the King's Bench to Warwickshire in 1387. The rolls prepared for the court's visit in 1397 (P.R.O.JUST2/189, 191) do not usually give the date of the inquest.

17.Hunnisett, *Medieval Coroner*, 122.

18.See above p.7.

19.*C.P.R. 1345-48*, 32.

20.C.C.A. BA/B/P/431/5.

21.C.C.A. BA/B/P/434/4.

22.*C.P.R.1345-48*, 32; *C.C.R. 1330-33*, 466-467; *C.C.R. 1333-37*, 475.

23.C.C.A. BA/H/H/278/24.

24.C.C.A. BA/B/P/351/7, BA/B/P/360/1. There are no references to Waller after this date so he probably died in the Black Death.

25.C.C.A. BA/H/H/5/1.

26.C.C.A. BA/B/P/14/32.

27.*C.P.R.1345-48*, 32.

28.P.R.O. JUST2/180.

29.P.R.O. JUST2/180.

30.C.C.A. BA/B/P/113/1.

31.P.R.O. JUST2/182 (tricesimo has been omitted before sexto for the regnal year at the head of this roll).

32.P.R.O. JUST2/182 m.2 dorse.

33.P.R.O. JUST3/142 m.19.

34.P.R.O. JUST3/142 m.15. (There is a transcript in H.R.C.C. I, f.175).

35.C.C.A. BA/B/P/175/34, BA/B/P/444/1, 3; *The Register of the Guild of the Holy Trinity*, 78.

36.*C.C.R. 1369-74*, 129.

37.C.C.A. BA/B/P/117/13, BA/B/P/64/1, BA/B/P/197/4.

38.P.R.O. JUST 3/159 m.12. Richard Bron of Abingdon who appeared before the Justices of Gaol Delivery on 19th July 1370 had been appealed earlier before Ocham as coroner.

39.P.R.O. JUST3/160 m.10; see p.22 & 102.

40.P.R.O. JUST3/173 m.23.

41.P.R.O. JUST3/173 m.23.

42.*R.W.C.S.P.*, 73, 74, 80, 83; C.C.A. BA/ B/P/205/3.

43.P.R.O. JUST2/189 mm.2-3 dorse. The heading of this roll states that it runs from the Conversion of St. Paul, 11 Richard II (25th January 1388) but the first inquest on it was held on a man found on Thursday before St. Matthew (Mathei) in the same regnal year (19th September 1387). The entries on the roll are copies from the original coroner's files and it is possible that the inquest was held on Thursday before St.Mathias (20th February 1388) and that the copyist wrote Mathei for Mathie.

44.P.R.O. JUST2/189 m.2.

45.Fined for brewing and selling ale in unsealed measures 10th December 1379, *R.W.C.S.P.*, 30.

46. P.R.O. JUST3/177 m.14 dorse.

47.P.R.O. JUST3/177 m.15.

48.*R.W.C.S.P.*, 83; Alice Beardwood (Ed.) *The Statute Merchant Roll of Coventry 1392-1416*, Dugdale Society XVII, (1939), 7,13,17.

49.P.R.O. JUST2/191 m.2. (There is a transcript in H.R.C.C. I, ff. 248-249).

50.This is the date given at the head of Attelburgh's roll (P.R.O. JUST 2/191 m.2).

51. The date given at the head of Houlond's roll (P.R.O. JUST2/191 m.4). The first entry on the roll is dated 2nd December 1393. (There is a transcript in H.R.C.C. I, ff.251-6).

52. P.R.O. JUST2/191 m.4.

53. C.C.A. BA/B/P/14/5.

54. P.R.O. JUST2/191 m.8 dorse. There is no heading to the roll and only one item on it. (There is a transcript in H.R.C.C. I, f.257).

55. Coss, *Early Records*, p.32, no.34.

56. C.C.A. BA/H/H/100/9, BA/B/P/439/5-6, BA/B/P/439/7, PA468/11/47, 142 (3), 219.

57. C.C.A. BA/B/P/184/2, BA/B/P/182/5, PA468/11/219.

58. C.C.A. BA/B/P/178/13-15.

59. C.C.A. BA/H/H/100/9, BA/D/BH/1/1.

60. C.C.A. BA/B/P/175/19, BA/B/P/175/25, 27, 28.

61. C.C.A. BA/B/P/138/5.

62. C.C.A. BA/G/F/28/4-5, BA/B/P/182/5, PA468/11/L25, 356, 142 (3) and (4).

63. C.C.A. BA/B/P/182/5; *C.A.D.* IV A6181.

64. C.C.A. BA/H/H/221/6.

65. P.R.O. CP40/313 rot.117 dorse; C.C.A. BA/B/P/404/1.

66. Coss, *Early Records,* nos. 307, 322.

67. *C.P.R. 1345-48*, 32.

68. C.C.A. Borough Archive deeds 1-22 Edw.III passim; PA468/11/L25, 142 (3) and (4), 356.

69.Transactions of the Midland Record Society V, Supplement, 7; *Lay Subsidy Roll, Warks. 1332*, 45.

70.*Reports from the Lord's Committees... touching the Dignity of a Peer 1820-29* IV, 566; C.C.A. BA/B/P/182/5; B.R.L. Ms. 377487.

71.C.C.A. PA468/11/142 (3).

72.*The Register of the Guild of the Holy Trinity*, 16, 22.

73.C.C.A. BA/B/P/189/1, BA/D/BH/1/2.

74.C.C.A. BA/B/P/189/1-2, BA/B/P/182/5, BA/D/BH/1/2, BA/B/P/175/31, BA/B/P/14/14. The donees of the cottage were Sewall de Bulkington, Nicholas de Baddesleye and Wm. le Themelere, for whom see notes 78 and 81.

75.C.C.A. BA/B/P/187/1. The donees were Sewall de Bulkington, Master of St. Mary's Guild (C.C.A. BA/B/P/242/2, BA/B/P/143/22), Wm. le Thumelere, Nicholas de Haytale, Thomas de Shepeye and John son of John de Rideware. The last four all appear in *The Register of the Guild of the Holy Trinity* (Dugdale Society XIII, 1935), 16, 51, 71, 82 and their positions near the head of the lists of members bearing their Christian names makes it almost certain that they were St. Mary's members.

76.C.C.A. BA/B/P/187/2. The chaplains were Adam de Ichyngton, named as chaplain to St. John the Baptist's Guild (C.C.A. BA/B/P/137/5), Wm. de Lalleford and John de Newenham. All three appear in *The Register of the Guild of the Holy Trinity*, pp. 1, 17, 85.

77. C.C.A. BA/H/H/243/1.

78.P.R.O. E40/A6181. Thos. de Merynton, Nicholas de Baddesleye and Henry de Lichfield. Baddesleye was chaplain of St. Mary's Guild (C.C.A. BA/B/P/242/2). Lichfield was associated with Baddesleye and Sewall de Bulkington, Master of the Guild, as trustees and lessors of guild property (C.C.A. BA/H/H/366/1, 3). Baddesleye and Lichfield appear in *The Register of the Guild of the Holy Trinity*, 10, 52.

79.C.C.A. BA/B/P/360/1.

80. C.C.A. BA/B/P/349/25; P.R.O. CP40/428 rot. xxxiiij.

81. Coss, *Early Records*, passim; C.C.A. BA/B/P/349/25-26, BA/H/H/278/14-15, BA/B/P/353/2, BA/B/P/359/1, BA/B/B/2/1; S.B.T. DR10/331, 342.

82. Coss, *Early Records*, no.33.

83. C.C.A. BA/B/B/2/1.

84. P.R.O. CP40/248 rot. xxxiiij, KB27/259 m.24 (rex). Wm. le Waller paid 4 shillings lay subsidy in 1327 *(Transactions of the Midlands Record Society V*, Supplement, 7). John did not pay then or in 1332 when he was abroad.

85. *C.C.R.1330-33*, 466-7, 498, 519. For the vacillations in English policy with regard to the Staple see Eileen Power, *The Wool Trade in English Medieval History* (Oxford 1941), 86 et seq.

86. *C.C.R.1333-37*, 475.

87. P.R.O. CP40/310 rot.99 dorse, CP40/313 rot.98 dorse.

88. E.g. *Index of Placita de Banco* (P.R.O. Lists and Indices XXXII) Pt. II, p. 685 ('Grove' = Grene); *Year Books of Edward II* vol. xxii (Selden Society vol. 61 (1942), 123-130; P.R.O. CP40/313 rot.40 dorse.

89. *C.C.R. 1330-33*, 467.

90. C.C.A. BA/B/P/15/2; *The Register of the Guild of the Holy Trinity*,15.

91. *C.P.R. 1345-48*, 32.

92. C.C.A. BA/B/P/351/7, BA/B/P/163/5, BA/B/P/360/1.

93. C.C.A. BA/B/B/2/1, BA/B/P/361/1. Wm. Luffe, Master in 1350 (C.C.A. BA/B/P/292/20-21, BA/B/P/292/13, BA/B/P/137/12, BA/B/P/188/2), Nich. de Baddesleye, chaplain of St. Mary's (C.C.A. BA/B/P/242/2, BA/B/P/137/12), Henry de Lichfield, chaplain, and Wm. de Taunton (*The Register of the Guild of the Holy Trinity*, 10, 83).

94.C.C.A. BA/H/H/186/1, Richard Frebern, Master 1352-53 (C.C.A. BA/B/P/14/2, BA/B/P/19/1).

95.C.C.A. BA/A/C/8/4.

96.*The Lay Subsidy Roll for Warwickshire, 1332*, 44-45.

97.P.R.O. E179/242/94.

98.*Year Book of Edw. III* (Rolls Series) Year 20 Pt. ii, 98-113, 573-7. C.C.A. BA/B/P/15/1 for the Box-Ballard relationship.

99.*Transactions of the Midland Record Society V*, Supplement, 7.

100.P.R.O. E101/121/7 mm.1 dorse, 2.

101.*The Register of the Guild of the Holy Trinity*, 78; C.C.A. BA/B/P/175/34, BA/B/P/444/1, 3; *Victoria County History of Warwickshire*, VIII, 157.

102.*C.C.R. 1369-74,129*. January 25th was the normal date for election of the mayor and coroner in Coventry.

103.Hunnisett, *Medieval Coroner*, 172-176.

104.C.C.A. BA/B/P/295/3, BA/B/P/14/14, BA/B/P/14/3.

105.See list of coroners, p.33.

106.E.g. C.C.A. BA/B/P/175/34, BA/H/H/8/2, BA/B/P/301/2.

107.C.C.A BA/B/P/444/1, 3.

108.The six are Thos. Baldeswell, John Houlond, Ralph Huitt, William de Ocham (see below), Roger Wedon and John Wyott.

109.E.g. Richard le Darker, a founder of St. Katherine's Guild, does not appear, although his wife Alice does *(The Register of the Guild of the Holy Trinity*, 3).

110. C.C.A. BA/B/P/250/1, BA/B/P/117/12-13, BA/B/P/17/15, BA/B/P/178/32, BA/B/P/301/2-3, BA/B/P/204/1-2, BA/B/P/197/4, BA/B/P/14/5.

111.*The Statute Merchant Roll of Coventry, 1392-1416*, 7, 13, 14, 17, 21, 60.

112.*The Statute Merchant Roll of Coventry, 1392-1416*, xvii-xix.

113.C.C.A. BA/B/P/201/2 (endorsement), BA/B/P/359/28; *The Statute Merchant Roll of Coventry, 1392-1416*, 49.

Chapter 4: The Jurors

1. P.R.O. JUST2/180.

2. P.R.O. JUST2/182.

3. 4817 Coventrians paid the Poll Tax in 1377 (W.G. Hoskins, *Local History in England*, 1972, p.238). All over 14 years of age were liable except beggars and beneficed clergy. Assuming that the sexes were about equal, and allowing for some evasion, there are likely to have been about 2500 males in 1377. In 1355 only six years after the Black Death and at an early stage in the development of the cloth industry, it is unlikely that there were more than 2000.

4. P.R.O JUST2/189 mm.2-3d; H.R.C.C. I, ff. 240-247.

5. *R.W.C.S.P.*, 5-84 passim.

6. P.R.O. JUST2/180, 182. It is not certain that the four mentions of John le Smyth refer to the same man.

7. P.R.O. JUST2/180 m.4; JUST2/182 m.1 dorse; P.R.O. E164/21 f.120.

8. P.R.O. E101/121/7 and JUST1/971 rot. 1 dorse.

9. *C.P.R. 1348-50*, 32.

10. C.C.A. Borough Archives deeds temp. Edw.III, passim.

11. P.R.O. JUST2/180 m.4.

12. C.C.A. BA/B/P/222/11.

13. P.R.O. JUST2/180 m.3; C.C.A. BA/H/H/150/4.

14. Putnam, *Enforcement of the Statutes of Labourers*, 372; P.R.O. JUST 2/180 m.1; JUST2/182 mm. 1 and 1 dorse. The owner of the White Cellar was Richard Frebern (C.C.A. BA/D/K/14/4).

15. List of mayors *(Coventry Municipal Handbook)*.

16. P.R.O. SC2/207/18 m.8.

17. P.R.O. JUST2/180 m.1; C.C.A. BA/H/H/366/1, BA/B/P/359/7, BA/B/P/242/2, BA/B/P/294/13,15, BA/B/P/143/22, BA/H/H/366/3, BA/B/A/69/7, BA/B/P/76/1, 2, BA/B/P/329/4, BA/B/P/141/19; *House of Lords Report ... on the Dignity of a Peer*, IV, 571.

18. P.R.O. JUST2/180 m.3 dorse. There were two Richard Freberns: the former bailiff and mayor was styled senior in 1352 when he was Master of St. Mary's Guild (C.C.A. BA/B/P/14/2) so it is possible that the juror in 1358 was the younger Richard.

19. Robt. le Thumelere, John le Seler and Wm. de Wendleburgh (P.R.O. JUST2/180 mm. 1, 3 dorse; *C.P.R. 1345-48*, 32), Richard Godeswowes, Henry de Kele, Adam de Keresleye, Robt. le Thumelere and Edward de Wedon (P.R.O. JUST2/180 mm. 1 dorse, 3, 3 dorse). The identification of the juror John de Norton with the merchant who had a rood in Cheylesmore Park in 1348 (P.R.O. JUST2/180 m. 1 dorse; *C.P.R. 1345-48, 32)* is uncertain as there was more than one of that name.

20. This paragraph is based on a correlation of the names of the jurors in P.R.O. JUST2/180 with the lists of those fined or presented in P.R.O. E101/121/7 and P.R.O. JUST1/971 rot. 1 dorse.

21. P.R.O. JUST2/180 mm. 1 and 3; P.R.O. E101/121/7 m.2; Putnam, *Enforcement of the Statutes of Labourers*, 372.

22. P.R.O. JUST2/180 mm. 1 and 1 dorse; P.R.O. JUST1/971 rot. 1 dorse.

23. P.R.O. JUST2/180 m.3 dorse; JUST3/167 mm. 23 dorse, 27 dorse; C.C.A. BA/B/P/14/3, 4, BA/B/P/403/7.

24. P.R.O. JUST2/180 m.1; *Feet of Fines for Warks.*, III no. 2217.

25. P.R.O. JUST2/180 m.4; C.P.R. 1356-58, 371; Sharpe, *Antiquities of Coventry*, 88; C.C.A. BA/B/P/441/1.

26. C.C.A. Borough Archive deeds 1-30 Edw.III, passim; *C.P.R. 1345-48*, 32.

27.P.R.O. JUST2/180 m.1 dorse; *C.P.R. 1361-64, 501*; C.C.A. BA/B/P/331/4; PA468/11/262; List of mayors *(Coventry Municipal Handbook)*; *R.W.C.S.P.*, 12-94. See note 18 above regarding Richard Frebern.

28.C.C.A. Borough Archive deeds 33, 34, 37, 38, 43-45 Edw.III; PA468/11/71, 94; P.R.O. JUST3/146 rot. 4 dorse; P.R.O. E315/38/94.

29.C.C.A. BA/B/P/242/2, BA/B/P/295/3.

30.P.R.O. JUST2/180 mm. 1, 1 dorse, 3 dorse.

31.P.R.O. JUST2/180 m.1. Whitemore appears as Whiteman in this jury list, but as Whitemore in two others on the same membrane.

32.C.C.A. BA/B/P/44/8, BA/H/H/301/5, 7, 8, 9; *C.P.R. 1354-58*, 372; Sharpe, *Antiquities*, 88.

33.Coss, *Early Records*, no. 375; Dugdale, W., *Antiquities of Warwickshire* (Ed. Thomas, 1730), 158.

34.Davis, *Early History*, 26-27.

35.Richardson H.G. and Sayles G.O. (Eds.), *Rotuli Parliamentorum ... inediti*, 256, 264.

36. Hunnisett, 'The Medieval Coroner' in, *American Journal of Legal History*, III, 214-5, 344.

Chapter 5: The Powers and Personnel of the Commission of the Peace

1.*Statutes of the Realm* I, 96-98. Also printed in W. Stubbs, *Select Charters*, 463-9.

2.H. Spelman, *Glossarium Archaiologicum* (London, 1664), 543-4; C.P.R.1307-13, 372.

3.E.g. *C.P.R.1307-13*, 87, 130, 170, 171, 549; *C.P.R.1313-17*, 56, 62-63, 67, 70, 71, 74, 236, 242.

4. Bertha H. Putnam, 'The Transformation of the Keepers of the Peace into Justices of the Peace 1327-1380', *Transactions of the Royal Historical Society* (4th Series) XII (1929), 19-48.

5.P.R.O. JUST2/180 m.3 dorse.

6.Statute 34 Edw.III cc. 1, 5, 6, 9-11, *Statutes of the Realm* I, 365-7.

7.Putnam, ut supra, 43-47; Statute 42 Edw.III c.6, *Statutes of the Realm* I, 388.

8.*R.W.C.S.P.* where the rolls are fully printed and analysed in more detail than is possible here; T.W. Whitley, *The Parliamentary Representation of the City of Coventry*, (Coventry, 1894), 20.

9.*C.Ch.R.* V, 380. In 1439 the Coventry J.P.s with their Recorder were commissioned to deliver Coventry gaol 'this time' (hac vice), which would involve trying felonies (H.R.C.C. I, 224).

10.*R.W.C.S.P.* lix-lxviii; A. Harding, *The Law Courts of Medieval England* (1973), 95.

11.Harding, *Law Courts*, 95.

12.Statute 42 Edw.III c.6, *Statutes of the Realm* I, 388.

13.*C.P.R.1354-58*, 62; *C.P.R.1358-61*, 420; *C.P.R. 1364-67*, 434;

C.P.R.1367-70, 194, 418; *C.P.R. 1370-74*, 478; *C.P.R.1374-77*, 313, 315; *C.P.R.1377-81*, 47, 515; *C.P.R. 1385-89*, 254; *C.P.R. 1391-96*, 587, 588; *C.P.R.1396-99*, 230, 240, 437.

14.*R.W.C.S.P.*, Appendix I, lxxxv - lxxxviii.

15.*C.C.R.1381-85*, 104; *R.W.C.S.P.*, xxvii-xxix, xliii, xci-xciii, 139-145, 151.

16.*R.W.C.S.P.*, xxxvi.

17.*C.P.R. 1391-96*, 587; *C.P.R. 1396-99*, 240; *R.W.C.S.P.*, xcii-xciv. But John of Gaunt, the King's uncle, on his way to the north in 1381, sat as a Warwickshire justice at the session on May 14th held in Coventry, perhaps for his convenience. No Coventry cases were tried and the Coventry justices held their usual session a week later (*R.W.C.S.P.*, xxx, xc, 102-4).

18.*C.P.R. 1354-58*, 62.

19.*Dictionary of National Biography* XXIII, 43; LII, 356.

20.List of mayors (*Coventry Municipal Handbook*).

21.R.A. Pelham, 'The Early Wool Trade in Warwickshire and The Rise of the Merchant Middle Class', *T.B.A.S.,1939-40*, (1944), 53-54; *C.P.R. 1327-30*, 313; P.R.O. E211/285 and 485; *C.A.D.* I, B1376; *C.A.D.* II, B3731; *C.A.D.* III, A4332; *C.A.D.* IV, A9442; *Feet of Fines for Warks.*, II, 1806, 1814, 1822, 1830, 1929; C.C.A. BA/H/H/100/10.

22.*The Register of the Guild of the Holy Trinity*, 1.

23.*C.P.R. 1343-45*, 490; *C.P.R. 1350-54*, 157; *C.F.R. 1337-47*, 97.

24.*C.P.R. 1350-54*, 201.

25.P.R.O. KB27/259 m.24 (Rex), printed in *Parliamentary Writs*, Vol. II, division II, Appendix, 269, and in Camden Society, Series I, Vol. 24, xxiii-xxix.

26.*C.P.R.1350-54*, 87, 92, 284, 449, 450; *C.P.R. 1354-58*, 59, 60, 62, 226, 294, 295, 387.

27.*C.P.R. 1350-54*, 201.

28.*C.P.R. 1350-54*, 275, 288, 332, 507, 515; *C.P.R.1354- 58*, 56, 63, 65, 68, 119, 125, 331, 334, 385, 454.

29.*C.P.R. 1354-58*, 99, 318.

30.P.R.O. E101/121/7 m.2 dorse.

31.*R.W.C.S.P.*, xlvii-xlviii.

32.They were William de Catesby (C.P.R. 1367-70, 191, 194), Richard de Stafford (P.R.O. JUST3/157 m.3 dorse) and Simon de Lichfield (*C.P.R. 1374-77*, 313; *R.W.C.S.P.*, xlvii). The references in brackets are for indications of their being leading justices or custos rotulorum. Their appointments outside Coventry can be found in the *Calendar of Patent Rolls* and the *Register of Edward the Black Prince*, Part IV (P.R.O. 1933).

33.*C.A.D.* III, A4523, A4276, A4312; *C.A.D.* IV, A7648, A10275; *C.A.D.* V, A10867, A10868, A11050, A12114; P.R.O. E42/162, 205; *Feet of Fines for Warks.*, III, 2031; C.C.A. BA/B/P/81/3, BA/B/P/328/11, 12.

34.C.C.A. BA/E/B/21/1
35.List of mayors (*Coventry Municipal Handbook*); commissions as in note 13 above.

36.*C.Ch.R. 1341-1417*, 380.

37.E.g. M.D. Harris, *The Coventry Leet Book*, 25.

38.E.g. P.R.O. JUST3/140 mm. 1-3, and elsewhere in the gaol delivery rolls.

39.*R.W.C.S.P.*, 15.

40.*C.P.R. 1364-67*, 434.

41.E.g. P.R.O. CP40/313, rots. 87 dorse, 99, 150 dorse. See also N.W. Alcock, 'The Catesbys in Coventry', *Midland History* XV (1990), 3-4, 032.

42. G.O. Sayles (ed.), '*Select Cases in the Court of the King's Bench under Edward III*', Selden Society (1965), 85.

43. *C.P.R. 1367-70*, 194, 418; *C.P.R. 1370-74*, 478.

44. *C.P.R. 1385-89*, 254; *C.P.R. 1388-92*, 136; *C.P.R. 1391-96*, 436, 587, 588; *C.P.R. 1396-99*, 228, 230, 238, 240, 370, 436, 437; T.W. Whitley, *The Parliamentary Representation of the City of Coventry*, 20; *R.W.C.S.P.*, xciii-xciv. The sessions rolls from 1387-99 are not continuous but Purefrey sat at every session of which the record survives.

45. *C.C.R. 1381-85*, 104.

46. *R.W.C.S.P.*, xcii-xciii, 139-43, 151.

47. *C.P.R. 1381-85*, 350.

48. *R.W.C.S.P.*, xcii-xciii. There are some gaps in the Warwickshire rolls for 1384-86.

49. *R.W.C.S.P.*, xciii-xciv, 62, 71-83; List of mayors (*Coventry Municipal Handbook*).

50. *R.W.C.S.P.*, lxxxix-xciv.

51. C.C.A. [updateE4 m.6]; *R.W.C.S.P.*, 67, 94; *C.P.R. 1385-89*, 254; *C.P.R. 1391-96*, 587.

52. *R.W.C.S.P.*, 94, 95, 126.

53. *C.Ch.R.* V, 241-243; M.D. Harris, *The Coventry Leet Book*, Plan of the County of Coventry (frontispiece).

54. C.C.A. BA/E/B/21/1; *R.W.C.S.P.*, 9, 53.

55. H.R.C.C. I, ff. 213-217.

56. H.R.C.C. I, f. 226v.

Chapter 6: The Jurors

1. *R.W.C.S.P.*, 5-85 for lists of jurors and constables; l-lv for a fuller analysis than is given here.

2. *R.W.C.S.P.*, 18, 50, 54, 59; List of mayors (*Coventry Municipal Handbook*). There is the possibility, of course, that it was a younger John Barowe who was mayor.

3. The others were Wm. de Cayfeld, bailiff in 1362, John Stowe (1380), Thos. Marchall (1388), Richard Marchall (1399), John Egeston (1405 and 1406), Adam Deyster (1412), Richard Palmere (1414). For their service as jurors see *R.W.C.S.P.*, 9, 18, 40, 46, 50, 54, 55, 59, 62, 71, 73, 74, 77, 78.

4. Wm. Lybard, bailiff in 1379, Richard de Duddeleye (1387), Adam Deyster (1412), Richard Power (1411), and Wm. de Eton (1413). For their service as constables see *R.W.C.S.P.*, 6, 12, 13, 15, 16, 19, 23.

5. John Stowe, Robt. Ingram, Hen. Draycote, Robt. Snayth, Richard de Shethesby, Thos. de Merston, Richard Peg, John Asteleye, Robt. de Estylton, Roger de Wedon, Walter Dawe, Wm. de Canleye, Robt. de Balsall, Wm. Lyberd junior, Wm. de Wednesbury, John Marshall, John Peuterer, John Inge, Raplh Coupere and Wm. de Norton (*R.W.C.S.P.*, 6, 9, 10, 14, 15, 16, 18, 20, 22, 23, 24, 29-31, 33, 36, 39-41, 45-47, 53-56, 59, 66).

6. *R.W.C.S.P.*, 23, 25, 27, 35, 49, 113, 114. A Wm. Brown, bellringer, was acquitted of theft in 1382 and a Wm. Brown (unstyled) was a juror in 1387, but there was a horner of the same name who was a constable in 1396-97.

7. *R.W.C.S.P.*, 14, 30-32.

8. *R.W.C.S.P.*, 7, 14, 34, 43.

9. *R.W.C.S.P.*, 12, 46, 50, 55.

Chapter 7:
The Justices of the Peace in Action

1.The indictments emanating from the jurors and constables were analysed at length by Dr. Kimball and Professor Plucknett (*R.W.C.S.P.*, lv-lxviii, 179-189).

2.*R.W.C.S.P.*, 25-26 (the name there printed as Lukell is revealed as Lifpull by ultra-violet light).

3.See *R.W.C.S.P.*, 188 for a long list of references to regrating.

4.E.g. *R.W.C.S.P.*, 6, 10, 13, 14, 20.

5.*R.W.C.S.P.*, 28.

6.E.g. M.D. Harris, *The Coventry Leet Book*, 25, 197, 272.

7.*R.W.C.S.P.*, 144.

8.*R.W.C.S.P.*, 38-40.

9.*R.W.C.S.P.*, 25, 29-32.

10.*R.W.C.S.P.*, 14, 30, 32.

11.*R.W.C.S.P.*, 59.

12.*R.W.C.S.P.*, 9.

13.*R.W.C.S.P.*, 65.

14.*R.W.C.S.P.*, lxxix-lxxxiii, 63; M. Dormer Harris, *Life in an Old English Town*, (London, 1898), 276-8.

15.*R.W.C.S.P.*, lvi-lix.

16.*R.W.C.S.P.*, 82.

17.*R.W.C.S.P.*, 71.

18.*R.W.C.S.P.*, 47.

19.*R.W.C.S.P.*, 12-13.

20.*R.W.C.S.P.*, 36.

21.See page 5 94-95.

22.*R.W.C.S.P.*, 45-46.

23.*R.W.C.S.P.*, 84-85.

24.See pages 43 and 55.

25.*R.W.C.S.P.*, 54.

26.*R.W.C.S.P.*, 11, 41.

27.*R.W.C.S.P.*, 58.

28.*R.W.C.S.P.*, 74-75.

29.See *R.W.C.S.P.*, 186-7 for a list.

30.*Rotuli Parliamentorum* III, 326.

31.K.B. McFarlane, 'Bastard Feudalism', *Bulletin of the Institute of Historical Research* XX, 173-4; *Dictionary of National Biography* II, 400.

32.*C.P.R. 1391-96*, 2.

33.Dugdale, *Antiquities of Warwickshire* (1730), 231.

34.*R.W.C.S.P.*, lxiii, 75-78; *C.P.R.1391-96*, 731.

35.*R.W.C.S.P.*, 61; P.R.O. JUST 3/167 m.40.

36.*R.W.C.S.P.*, lvi-lviii, lx, 181-182, 185.

37.*R.W.C.S.P.*, 24, 36.

38.*R.W.C.S.P.*, 26-27.

39.*R.W.C.S.P.*, 8, 19, 27, 42, 49, 80.

40.*R.W.C.S.P.*, 40-43.

41.In 1399 a commission of oyer and terminer was appointed to enquire about false coinings in Coventry and its suburbs. The commissioners were two judges, Geoffrey de Hampton (mayor), Thos. Purefrey (recorder) and Richard Clerk (ex-mayor). (*C.P.R. 1396-99*, 512).

42.*R.W.C.S.P.*, 65. A small amount (20d), but perhaps they were indicted as a warning to others.

43.*R.W.C.S.P.*, 64.

44.*R.W.C.S.P.*, 145. Somenour was indicted before the Warwickshire justices as the Coventry commission of the peace was suspended.

45.*R.W.C.S.P.*, 28, 149-150; *C.P.R. 1385-89*, 416; P.R.O. KB27/508 rex m. 6 dorse.

46.*R.W.C.S.P.*, 49-51. It was not only ecclesiastical officials who indulged in extortion; the under sheriff of Warwickshire, Wm. Ladbrok, imprisoned James de Bevynton, the former mayor of Coventry and extracted 100s for his release (*R.W.C.S.P.*, 96).

47.*R.W.C.S.P.*, 17.

48.*R.W.C.S.P.*, 73.

49.*R.W.C.S.P.*, 39.

50.4817 people paid the poll tax in 1377 (W.G. Hoskins, *Local History in England* (1972), 238). No doubt there were evasions, but a round figure of 5000 is not unlikely to be far out. Tax was levied on individuals aged fourteen and over, and a multiplier of 1.5 has been suggested to estimate the total population (J.C. Russell, *British Medieval Population*,

Alberquerque, U.S.A., 1948, 142-143).

51. *R.W.C.S.P.*, lvi, lxxxix-xciv. All the figures given for 14th century offences in the following paragraphs, except those from the Coroners' Rolls, are from Dr. Kimball's Introduction lv-lxviii, and Professor Plucknett's totals on pp. 180-7 of the same volume, and refer to indictments.

52. All crime statistics for 1988 are from the *Annual Report of the Chief Constable of the West Midlands for 1988*, p.135, Table A.

53. P.R.O. JUST2/180, 182, 191.

54. P.R.O. JUST2/180 mm.1, 1 dorse, 3; JUST2/189 m.2 dorse; JUST2/191 mm.3 dorse, 4.

55. P.R.O. JUST2/180 mm.1, 1 dorse, 4; JUST2/182 m.2; JUST2/191m.2.

56. P.R.O. JUST2/180, passim; JUST2/182 mm. 1, 2; JUST2/198 mm. 2, 3; JUST2/191 mm.2, 2 dorse, 6, 7.

57. P.R.O. JUST2/180 m.3 dorse.

58. *R.W.C.S.P.*, lxvi-lxvii. The results of the trials of seven suspects are not known. We have assumed that those put in exigend (the first stage of outlawry) were outlawed.

59. *R.W.C.S.P.* , 120, 131, 147.

60. *R.W.C.S.P.*, lxvii.

61. P.R.O. JUST3/140 m.3.

Chapter 8: The Justices of Labourers

1.Ordinance printed from the Close Rolls in Bertha H. Putnam, *The Enforcement of the Statutes of Labourers ... 1349-1359* (New York, 1908), 8-11; and in *Statutes of the Realm* (1810-1828) Vol. I, 307-8. For the statute, ibid., 311-3.

2.P.R.O. E368/131 m.315.

3.*C.P.R. 1354-58*, 60.

4.P.R.O. E101/121/7, partly printed in Putnam, 371. Notes will not be given for further references to this document. No subsidy was being collected in 1355 so the Crown got the 'excesses' as well but they do not appear on this list.

5.P.R.O. JUST1/971 rot. 1 dorse. Notes will not be given for further references to this document.

6.Thomas Trayvill and Robert le Werkman alias Thatcher.

7.PRO SC2/207/18 m.2 dorse.

8.*C.P.R. 1354-58*, 372.

9.Teynton was one of the mainpernors for de la More.

10.C.C.A. BA/B/A/41/2, BA/H/H/346/2.

11.C.C.A. BA/B/A/68/2, BA/H/H/108/5, 6.

12. Putnam, 186-190.

13.John Robyns, active 1340-49, probably a member of the short-lived Guild of the Holy Cross; C.C.A.BA/H/H/278/23, BA/B/P/44/8, BA/H/H/301/4,5,6,8,9,10.

14.In C.C.A. Borough Archive deeds (BA) and Drapers' deeds (PA468); S.B.T. Gregory Hood deeds, and Coventry deeds in P.R.O.

15. Jurors named in P.R.O. JUST2/180, 182.

16. P.R.O. JUST2/180 mm.1, 2, 4.

17. Hugh le Webbe acquired Viel's quarry in 1335 (C.C.A. BA/H/H/300/6,7).

18. C.C.A. BA/H/H/219/3,4,5.

19. List in *C.P.R. 1348-50, 32*; original deed (14th June 1347) C.C.A. BA/G/A/2/4.

20. *R.W.C.S.P.*, 25.

21. P.R.O. JUST3/142 rot.28. Tonour was not connected with Coventry.

22. P.R.O. JUST2/182 m.1.

23. P.R.O. JUST2/182 m.2; P.R.O. C260/78/2.

24. *R.W.C.S.P.*, 17.

25. Henri-E. de Sagher, 'L'Immigration des Tisserands Flamands et Brabancons en Angleterre', *Melanges d'Histoire Offerts a Henri Pirenne* (Brussels, 1926), 15-16.

26. R.A. Pelham, 'Cloth Markets of Warwickshire during the later Middle Ages', *T.B.A.S.* LXVI (for 1945-46), (1950), 135.

27 *R.W.C.S.P.*, passim; *The Register of the Guild of the Holy Trinity*, 3, 40.

28. C.C.A. BA/H/H/301/14.

29. C.C.A. PA468/D11/49.

30. *The Register of the Guild of the Holy Trinity*, 30, 75.

31. C.C.A. BA/B/P/178/51, 53.

32. P.R.O. JUST1/971, writs attached to rot.2.

33. C.C.A. BA/B/P/178/51, 53.

34. C.C.A. Borough Archives deeds 30 Edw.III passim; P.R.O. JUST2/182.

35. C.C.A. Borough Archives deeds 24 and 26 Edw.III passim.

36. C.C.A. BA/B/P/441/1.

37. C.C.A. BA/E/B/21/1, PA468/D11/47, deed attached to no.206, 208.

38. *C.P.R. 1354-58*, 371; C.C.A. BA/B/P/175/33, BA/B/P/82/1.

39. C.C.A. BA/B/P/178/21, BA/H/H/176/4, BA/B/P/192/1.

40. C.C.A. BA/D/AG/2/2, PA468/D11/97; S.B.T. DR10/356.

41. C.P.R. 1348-50, 32.

42. There seem to have been two men called John de Wedon, so we cannot be sure that the latoner who bought a rood in 1348 was the employer of an *ancilla* in 1357.

43. H.L. Gray, 'The Production and Exportation of English Woollens in the Fourteenth Century', *English Historical Review* XXXIX (1924), 30, 34; R.A. Pelham, 'Cloth Markets of Warwickshire during the later Middle Ages', *T.B.A.S.* LXVI (for 1945-46), (1950), 132-3.

44. Coss, *Early Records*, xl.

45. M.D. Harris, *The Coventry Leet Book*, 246-247. The Drapers craft ranked second to the Mercers but may have had more members.

46. Mainly from deeds.

47. Coss, *Early Records*, 45-46. Twenty years later, three of these mercers, Robert de Stone, Hugh de Meryngton and Ralph le Hunte, were eminent wool merchants (*English Historical Review* XXXI (1916), 603).

48.C.C.A. BA/B/P/294/9; R.A. Pelham, 'The Early Wool Trade in Warwickshire and the Rise of the Merchant Middle Class', *T.B.A.S.*1939-40, 58-59.

49.1393 John Northwode, mercer, and 1398 John Preston, draper. For their trades see E. and A. Gooder (eds.) *The Pittancer's Rental* (University of Birmingham Department of Extramural Studies, 1973), 9, 10.

50.C.C.A. BA/B/P/295/3; Borough Archive deeds 38 Edw.III passim; P.R.O. *Calendar of Inquisitions, Miscellaneous 1348-77*, 394.

51.*C.P.R. 1334-38*, 481; *C.P.R. 1350-54*, 535; *C.C.R. 1337-39*, 148, 269; *C.C.R.1343-46*, 152, 464; R.A. Pelham, 'The Early Wool Trade in Warwickshire and the Rise of the Merchant Middle Class', 43.

52.P.R.O. SC2/207/19 m.1.

53.C.C.A. BA/B/P/142/1, BA/B/P/184/1, 2, BA/H/H/100/10, BA/B/C/1/1, PA468/D11/93; S.B.T. DR10/328, 329.

54.*Victoria County History, Warwickshire* VI, 30-32, 34, 78-81, 85, 147, 148, 187-190, 205.

55.*C.P.R. 1343-45*, 40; *C.P.R. 1358-61*, 257; C.C.A. BA/B/P/349/23, BA/H/H/10/2, Borough Archives deeds 28 Edw.III passim.

56.*C.C.R.1346-49*, 361-2; *C.C.R. 1364-68*, 198; *C.P.R. 1361-64*, 526; *Reports from the Lords' Committees... Touching the Dignity of a Peer,* (1820-29) IV, 571, 610.

57. *C.P.R. 1361-64*, 526; C.C.A. Borough Archives deeds 37 Edw.III passim; BA/B/P/14/3.

58.Richard Stoke, Henry Dilcock, William de Hapsford, in addition to those mentioned in the text.

59.*C.P.R. 1348-50*, 97-98; *Feet of Fines for Warks* III, no. 2032; *C.A.D.* V, A11564 is his will.

60.*C.P.R. 1343-45*, 40.

61.C.C.A. BA/B/P/441/1.

62.B.R.L. Ms. 377487.

63.C.C.A. Borough Archives deeds 29 Edw.III passim.

64.C.C.A. Borough Archives deeds 30 Edw.III passim.

65.C.C.A. Borough Archive deeds 26 Edw.III passim; BA/H/H/9/1.

66.C.C.A. BA/A/C/8/4, Borough Archives deeds 32 Edw.III passim.

67.C.C.A. BA/H/H/300/6, 7.

68.Putnam, 85-86.

69.P.R.O. E368/131 m.315.

70.C.C.A. BA/B/P/178/21, BA/H/H/176/4, BA/B/P/354/5.

71.C.C.A. BA/B/P/405/1, 2, PA468/D11(b).

72.C.C.A. PA468/5/3/55/10, PA468/5/3/31/1.

73.P.R.O. E101/121/7 m.2 dorse for fines by the J.P.s.

74.P.R.O. JUST3/146 m.3 dorse.

75.P.R.O. SC2/207/17 m.3 dorse.

76.*R.W.C.S.P.*, 9, 23, 25, 27, 28, 35.

77.Eileen Gooder, *Coventry's Town Wall* (Historical Association, Coventry Branch, 1971), 12, 14.

78. P.R.O. SC2/207/18 m.6.

79. P.R.O. C88/51/23.

Chapter 9: Cheylesmore Courts

1.P.R.O. JUST2/180, 182, 189, 191.

2.*R.W.C.S.P.*, 1-87.

3.*Register of Edward the Black Prince* Part IV, 261, 262.

4.R.H.C. Davis, *The Early History of Coventry*, 24, 25; P.R.O. SC2/207/17, 18, 19 passim. The three weeks court normally met at Cheylesmore, but when its meetings coincided with the court leet, they were held at Wolfpitlidyate (see e.g. P.R.O. SC2/207/18 m.3).

5.*Register of Edward the Black Prince* Part IV, 270, 310. Pakynton's widow was suing the abbot of Coombe from 19th October 1364 (P.R.O. SC2/207/18 m.3 et seq.), but the case may have started earlier as some court rolls are missing.

6.P.R.O. JUST3/142 m.16; H.R.C.C. I, f. 175v.

7.P.R.O. SC2/207/17-23.

8.P.R.O. SC2/207/17 m.6, SC2/207/18 m.4. In January 1359 Botiler had been allowed to defer his homage and fealty for Exhall until the following May (*Register of Edward the Black Prince* Part IV, 275-6).

9.P.R.O. SC2/207/17 m.5, SC2/207/19 m.1 dorse.

10.P.R.O. SC2/207/17, 18.

11.*Victoria County History, Warwickshire*, VIII, 86; P.R.O. SC2/207/17 mm.1, 6 dorse.

12.*Register of Edward the Black Prince* Part IV, 531; P.R.O. SC2/207/18 m.6. Sutton was a surety for Thomas's widow when she had charge of their daughter in 1380 (*C.I.P.M.* XV, 94, 95).

13.P.R.O. SC2/207/17 m.1, SC2/207/22 m.3.

14. P.R.O. SC2/207/17 mm.1 dorse - 3.

15. *Register of Edward the Black Prince* Part IV, 342.

16. P.R.O. SC2/207/17 m.4 dorse.

17. P.R.O. SC2/207/18 mm.1 dorse and 3.

18. P.R.O. SC2/207/22 m.2. There is a transcript of this in H.R.C.C. I, ff. 154-6.

19. P.R.O. SC2/207/23 m.2 dorse; H.R.C.C. I, f.159v.

20. P.R.O. SC2/207/22 mm.3 - 3 dorse.

21. Adam de Keresley, Ralph Hunt, Edward Weedon and William Cayville.

22. E.g. Ralph Hunt did suit 'for his foreign holding, outside the borough' *(tenur' extra Burgum forinsec')*.

23. P.R.O. SC2/207/18 m.4.

24. P.R.O. SC2/207/17 m.1.

25. P.R.O. SC2/197/79.

26. P.R.O. SC2/207/17 mm.1, 5.

27. P.R.O. SC2/207/18 m.4; SC2/207/19 m.8 dorse.

28. P.R.O. SC2/207/17 m.6.

29. P.R.O. SC2/207/17 m.2.

30. P.R.O. SC2/207/17 m.1 dorse.

31. P.R.O. SC2/207/17 m.3.

32. P.R.O. SC2/207/18 m.3 dorse.

33.W. Holdsworth, *A History of the English Law* III (1935), 674-5.

34.Atherstone died before February 1364 (*C.P.R. 1361-64*, 526), and it is only in the earlier court rolls that his name is given. Afterwards the defendant is the abbot of Coombe.

35.*Sic*. One would have expected *alias* before *pluries*.

36.P.R.O. SC2/207/17 mm.1 - 5 dorse.

37.P.R.O. SC2/207/17 m.6 et seq.; SC2/207/18 passim; SC2/207/19 passim.

38.See e.g. C.C.A. BA/B/P/178/21,23, BA/H/H/176/4; *Register of Edward the Black Prince* Part IV, 271-2.

39.P.R.O. SC2/207/19-22 passim.

40.P.R.O. SC2/207/18 m.3 et seq., SC2/207/19 passim.

41.P.R.O. SC2/207/18 m.4.

42.P.R.O. SC2/207/19 m.1.

43.Income from perquisites of court 36 Edw.III, 59s 4d; 48 Edw.III, £7 3s 7d, including 16s 3d for a stray animal. These amounts probably include income from the view of frankpledge (P.R.O. SC2/207/17 m.7, SC2/207/22 m.12).

44.In 1295 the Prior of Coventry's bailiff claimed on his behalf jurisdiction of a plea of debt brought against a Coventrian in the Knightlow hundred court. The claim was at first contested by the bailiff of Roger Montalt (successor to the earls of Chester) on the grounds that the defendent held of Montalt by knight service. This proves that the Prior was claiming jurisdiction in that pasrt of Coventry which had been in the earl's liberty, and which had been conveyed to him in 1250 by the Montalts who reserved for themselves the service of those holding by military tenure. (Robert C. Palmer, *The County Courts of Medieval England, 1150-1350* (Princeton, N.J. , 1982), 106n.).

45.The records are the 'fines' (final concords) whereby property was conveyed, to be found in C.C.A dispersed among the Borough Archive deeds, and the records of an assize of novel disseisin in G.O. Sayles (ed.), *Select Cases in the Court of the King's Bench* VI (Selden Society 82, 1965), 84-85.

46.Robert C. Palmer, *The County Courts*, 254.

47.P.R.O. CP40/411 rot. xxvij.

48.P.R.O. SC2/207/17 m.6. On the use of the writ *accedes recordari* see Robert C. Palmer, *The County Courts*, 276. The text of the writ on the Cheylesmore roll corresponds with that in Elas de Haas and G.D. Hall (eds.), *Early Registers of Writs* (Selden Society 87, 1970), 216, no. 216) plus the cause clause as on p.156, no.191.

49.P.R.O. SC2/207/18 m.5 dorse.

50.P.R.O. SC2/207/19 m.9.

51.C.C.A. BA/B/A/1/1

52.P.R.O. SC2/207/18 m.3.

53.*The Coventry Leet Book*, 326.

54.P.R.O. SC2/207/18 mm.6-9. For Webb's quarry see C.C.A. BA/H/H/300/6, 7. He was pledge for the fines imposed by the Justices of Labourers on John and Thomas Quareour (P.R.O.E101/121.7m2)

55.P.R.O. SC2/207/18 mm.5 dorse.

56.P.R.O. SC2/207/17 mm.3 and 3 dorse.

57.P.R.O. SC2/207/19 m.1.

58.P.R.O. SC2/207/19 mm.1 and 1 dorse.

59.C.C.A. BA/B/P/362/1, 2.

60. C.C.A. BA/B/P/222/1, 3.

61. P.R.O. SC2/207/18 m.2.

62. *Pied poudreux* (dusty foot), i.e. immediate judgement for itinerant merchants.

63. P.R.O. SC2/207/20 m.11.

64. We have so far failed to find any expansion of pipull' in the glossaries, and have assumed that it is a variant of *piperarius*, a spicer.

65. *C.A.D.* IV, A9785.

66. *The Register of the Guild of the Holy Trinity*, 17.

67. P.R.O. E42/175, E327/379; C.C.A. PA468 D11/41; S.B.T. DR10/356.

68. P.R.O. SC2/207/19 m.1 dorse.

69. P.R.O. SC2/207/18 mm.9, 9 dorse.

70. P.R.O. SC2/207/18 mm. 1 and 3.

71. P.R.O. SC2/207/19 mm. 1, 1 dorse.

72. P.R.O. SC2/207/18 m.8 dorse. Hamslape is described as a founder in SC2/207/19 m.1.

73. H.R.C.C. I, f. 172.

74. H.R.C.C. I, f. 175v (assuming that the indictment before the Black Prince's steward would be at the court leet).

75. P.R.O. SC2/207/23 m.12 dorse; H.R.C.C. I, ff. 160v, 161.

76. See *R.W.C.S.P.* especially pp. xlv-xlvi, lv-lxviii, 180-9.

77. *C. Ch. R.* V, 39.

78. P.R.O. SC2/207/18 mm. 1, 1 dorse, 2, 6 dorse, 8; SC2/207/19 mm. 2 and 2 dorse; SC2/207/20 mm. 2, 2 dorse, 6 and 6 dorse; SC2/207/21 mm.2, 2 dorse, 11 and 11 dorse; SC2/207/22 mm.1, 1dorse, 3, 4 and 4 dorse; SC2/207/23 mm.2, 2 dorse, 12 and 12 dorse; H.R.C.C. I, ff.147-152, 158-161v.

79. P.R.O. SC2/207/20 m.2; H.R.C.C. I, f. 147v-148.

80. P.R.O. SC2/207/20 m.2; H.R.C.C. I, f. 147v.

81. P.R.O. SC2/207/20 m.2; H.R.C.C. I, f. 147.

82. P.R.O. SC2/207/23 m.12 dorse; H.R.C.C. I, ff. 160v, 161.

83. P.R.O. SC2/207/23 m.12; H.R.C.C. I, f.160v.

84. P.R.O. SC2/207/22 mm.1, 1 dorse; H.R.C.C. I, ff.150-151v.

85. P.R.O. SC2/207/18 m.1 dorse.

86. P.R.O. SC2/207/23 mm.2, 12 dorse; H.R.C.C. I, ff. 159, 161.

87. P.R.O. SC2/207/22 m.1; H.R.C.C. I, f.150.

88. P.R.O. SC2/207/18 m.2.

89. P.R.O. SC2/207/20 m.2 dorse; H.R.C.C. I, f.149.

90. P.R.O. SC2/207/20 m.2 dorse; H.R.C.C. I, f.148v.

91. P.R.O. SC2/207/23 m. 12; H.R.C.C. I, f.160v.

92. P.R.O. SC2/207/23 m.12; H.R.C.C. I, f.160.

93. P.R.O. SC2/207/18 mm.2, 4; H.R.C.C. I, f.148.

94. P.R.O. SC2/207/23 m.2; H.R.C.C. I, f.158.

95. P.R.O. SC2/207/23 m.12 dorse.

96. *C.Ch.R.* V, 39-40, 242, 380.

97.P.R.O. SC2/207/23 m.2 dorse; H.R.C.C. I, f.159v.

98.P.R.O. SC2/207/22 m.1 dorse; H.R.C.C. I, f.152.

99.P.R.O. SC2/207/22 m.1 dorse; H.R.C.C. I, f.152. This court, unusually, was held at Cheylesmore.

100. P.R.O. SC2/207/18 mm. 1, 1 dorse, 2, 8; SC2/207/19 m.2; SC2/207/22 m.3.

101.C.C.A. PA468/11/71.

102.See e.g. P.R.O. SC2/207/18 m.2 where amongst others, Ralph le Hunte, Walter Whitewebbe, John de Meryngton and Andrew de Napton were fined.

103.C.C.A. [Corp manorial records Cheylesmore Manor Frankpledge Roll for 14 Oct 5 Hen VII - BA/G/A/6/3. All the known Cheylesmore Rolls for the 15th and 16th centuries are in C.C.A.

104.C.C.A. [Cheylesmore Manorial Records BA/G/A/24/1 account of John Stallworth, bailiff 11-12 Hen VI.

105.*The Coventry Leet Book*, 326.

106.A. and E. Gooder, Coventry before 1355, *Midland History*, VI 1981, p.10-12.

107.*The Coventry Leet Book*, passim.